Start Now. Get Perfect Later.

Start Now. Get Perfect Later.

*How to Make Smarter, Faster & Bigger Decisions
& Banish Procrastination*

ROB MOORE

First published in the UK in 2018 by John Murray Learning
First published in the US in 2018 by Nicholas Brealey Publishing
An imprint of John Murray Press

An Hachette company

1

British Library Cataloguing-in-Publication Data
A catalogue record for this book is available from the British Library.

ISBN (UK) 9781473685437
ISBN (US) 9781473690486
eBook ISBN (UK) 9781473685444
eBook ISBN (US) 9781473690059
Audio ISBN 9781473685413

Every reasonable effort has been made to trace copyright holders, but if there are any errors
or omissions, Nicholas Brealey will be pleased to insert the appropriate acknowledgement
in any subsequent printings or editions.

Printed and bound in Great britain by Clays Ltd, Elcograf S.p.A.

John Murray Press policy is to use papers that are natural, renewable and recyclable products
and made from wood grown in sustainable forests. The logging and manufacturing processes
are expected to conform to the environmental regulations of the country of origin.

Nicholas Brealey Publishing
John Murray Press
Carmelite House
50 Victoria Embankment
London, EC4Y 0DZ, UK
Tel: 020 3122 6000

Nicholas Brealey Publishing
Hachette Book Group
Market Place Center
53 State Street
Boston, MA 02109, USA
Tel: (617) 263 1834

www.nicholasbrealey.com

Contents

Section 3: Banish overwhelm & Start Now

Section 4: To do, or not to do?

Section 5: Who's the easiest person to lie to...?

Section 6: Research (75%). Test. Review. Tweak. Repeat. (Scale.)

6.1: Research

6.2: Test

6.3: Review. Tweak. Repeat. (Scale.)

Section 7: How to make faster, better, harder decisions

Section 8: Commitments

SECTION I

Introduction

Start now. Get perfect later. Just do it. End of book.

...If that were all it took, this book wouldn't be needed. You mostly know what to do, so why don't you just do it?

The ironic purpose of this book is to get you to do what you know you've got to do, and you need to do, yet you need to read a book to tell you to go and do it!

To add to the irony, I've thought about writing this book for years. I thought I was quite decisive, but now I'm not sure. I did 17 different things to put off writing the book so I'd feel better in the moment, only to feel frustrated as I got further behind and closer to the deadline.

In the end, I used the tricks that can be found in Chapter 34 back on myself, as some kind of sado-masochistic pleasure–pain paradox. If you're reading this book, it worked. Writing a book is a big, hard thing and, without a huge reason to get it done, I may have let myself off the hook. Most people have a book in them, the thing is it is still in them.

You become a Jedi Master of all methods of self-delusional procrastination and overwhelm when writing a book. So in reading *Start Now. Get Perfect Later*, not only will you learn how banish procrastination, and to make smarter, faster and bigger decisions, you'll also be taken on a journey of voyeurism through all my personal struggles writing my 10th book. On the outside it may look easy, having written nine books before, but the journey of battling with my 'inner bas-tard'* (official terminology) is the same. I guess I just know how to put it back in its box from time to time now.

I (finally) decided to write this book because underneath property, business, art and money, all subjects of books and companies I have operated past and present, indecision lurks and overwhelm stalks. Whether you're creative or commercial, a zero-aire or billionaire, a master or a disaster, you will always have to face these demons. I used to think decisions would get easier as I got better, but I was wrong. One property managed or over 700, no books written or 10, no world records or three, deep in debt or making millions, I found that decisions just get bigger and more important.

I used to wish it were easier, but soon learned I needed to get better. At any time, age or level of experience and wisdom, you can make a good decision that elevates you and a bad one that humbles you. I wanted to write a book that everyone could get benefit from; whether you're an entrepreneur who listens to my podcasts, or a property investor in our Progressive community, or you picked up this book on the off chance. Personally and professionally, socially and financially, making smarter, faster and harder decisions to banish procrastination and overwhelm will serve you well. Through this book, I hope to serve you well, for better health, wealth, happiness and decisiveness. And on the subject of decisiveness:

After studying over 500 millionaires, including Andrew Carnegie, Henry Ford, and Charles M. Schwab, journalist and author Napoleon Hill found that they shared a single quality: decisiveness. 'Analysis of several hundred people who had accumulated fortunes well beyond the million dollar mark disclosed

---

* 'inner bas-tard' - you'll meet my inner bas-tard later, and maybe your own too.

the fact that *every one of them* had the habit of reaching decisions promptly,' Hill wrote in his 1937 classic, *Think and Grow Rich*.

In addition to making decisions quickly and confidently, they also change decisions, if and when needed to, *slowly*, Hill noted. On the flip side, 'Those who reach decisions promptly and definitely know what they want, and generally get it… The world has the habit of making room for the man whose words and actions show that he knows where he is going. People who fail to accumulate money, without exception, have the habit of reaching decisions, if at all, very slowly, and of changing these decisions quickly and often.'

Whether you want to be a millionaire (inflation-adjusted million is in fact around £64 million in today's money), or not is neither here nor there. Being better at making faster, better, bigger and harder decisions will help you:

1 Get more done in less time
2 Battle less with analysis-paralysis and second-guessing yourself all the time
3 Improve your general confidence
4 Be a better parent and husband or wife
5 Find the ideal partner
6 Align with the right people in your life (staff, friends, partners)
7 Free up time to do more of what you love
8 Train yourself to make continually better, bigger and harder decisions, faster and more intuitively
9 Quieten your mind and help you stress and worry less
10 Maintain a healthy body and mind and live longer

Oh, and did I say it will make you more money?

So let's Start Now.

I

You are not a procrastinator, but…

'I'm a procrastinator', you may say to yourself. Maybe even in public? Like it's some kind of badge of honour you wear like swimming badges stitched into your Speedos. Like you can look at your DNA under a microscope and see the 'procrastinator' gene.

Be careful what you label yourself. What you think about, you bring about and what you name yourself, you'll blame yourself.

'I always procrastinate.' 'I'm never decisive (I think).'

There's no need to take on the 'identity' of 'being' a procrastinator, because actually that's a lie. The reality for every single one of us is that we are very decisive in areas where we are confident and experienced. Lionel Messi knows exactly when to shoot without asking for permission from his teammates. Lewis Hamilton knows when to brake without scheduling it in his diary. Nelson Mandela knew how to forgive without putting it on his 'to do' list.

They have the knowledge and intuition to call upon and carry forward. They just know, because they've been there many times before. The 'decision muscle' has been built, exercised and stress-tested over time. And so it is with you, in your areas of skill, focus and experience. The better you are, and the more memory of previous success you have, the more instinctive and accurate your decision-making is.

Until you start something new.

Maybe Messi wouldn't be as decisive in a ballet class? Maybe Mandela would have procrastinated over pulling the trigger of a gun? And maybe you are struggling with indecisiveness in some areas. But that doesn't identify and render you 'indecisive'. You wouldn't want a teacher to label your child 'stupid' just because they don't like science, so don't do the same to yourself.

Every human being possesses and expresses every human trait. As such you are not 'unmotivated' or 'lazy' either. You simply 'do' these traits when you are not engaged, interested, things get hard or the task at hand simply isn't important enough to you. You're the opposite when you're doing what you love and loving what you do.

Like a good football team on a run of bad form, decisiveness goes down when things don't go your way. But form is temporary and class is permanent. If you can be decisive in one area of your life, you can take that experience into all areas of your life. If fear and failure reduce it, then progress and success increase it.

Start Now sound bite

You are not a procrastinator, but you do it sometimes. Don't label yourself; model the best parts of yourself. If you are decisive in one area, you can be so in any area. Simply build your decision muscle by drawing on past decisive successes.

2

What are indecisiveness & procrastination?

'I'm taking care of my procrastination once and for all, just you wait and see.'

Have you ever had the overwhelming urge to do something completely and utterly random and useless in the name of avoiding important things?

As I was writing the last chapter (which is only two pages), I had the most overwhelming, all-body-and-mind-consuming urge to break down some boxes in my boardroom and put them in the skip. My life's calling right there, like a lightning bolt in my soul. Yes! I must break. Down. Boxes. (A job I've never done in my life.) Right now, in the name of salvation and humanity. Funny that I have not had this urge in the last 38 years, but all of a sudden when it is 'book writing time', it hits me!

And at risk of sounding even more crazy, I tried to justify this most important task by suggesting to myself to listen to a book on procrastination to research the book I was procrastinating on!

Before you judge me, we all have our own versions of this. Some will be habitual, and some will be one-off-random. Maybe you'll need a spontaneous haircut? Maybe you'll just have to go shopping (again)? Or be compelled to clean out the fridge immediately?

'Doing nothing is not as easy as it looks. You have to be careful because the idea of doing anything which could easily lead to doing something that could cut into your nothing and that would force me to have to drop everything'

Jerry Seinfeld

But it can be more serious. At least in this instance you are doing something to procrastinate away from. The sly one that creeps up on you from behind is the urge to 'get everything ready' *before* you start. 'Oh look, the house needs a good spring clean. The office needs re-arranging and all the paper filing. I really must make the bed right now. I'll change the sheets while I'm at it. And collapse more boxes because the skip will be gone soon and I'll miss my only chance ever to do this life-balancing task.' This is called 'pre-crastination' and will be dealt with in Chapter 8, as will the weird and wonderful reasons for doing these mundane tasks like your life depended on it.

Indecisiveness and procrastination come in many hidden forms. Perhaps you simply have a hard time making general decisions? Or harder ones? You might make a decision but then endlessly question it afterwards, never fully backing yourself or your decision. You might chop and change your mind a lot? You may be vague, hesitant or lack clarity and conviction? Even the smallest decisions like where to go for dinner might frazzle your brain?

We procrastinate when we fear a threat to our sense of worth and independence, as a method of avoiding difficult situations. We procrastinate when a task could consume much needed energy for more useful (survival-based) functions. Procrastination is not an illness, disease or identity (crisis), it is a self-protection mechanism that has a very useful purpose, if somewhat outdated. Sometimes it does such a good job at getting us to do nothing, that we do nothing. Let's move on to why you (we) procrastinate so you can get a deep understanding and context on which to make good decisions, because sometimes procrastination is a good thing.

Start Now sound bite

Procrastination and indecisiveness are normal human traits that serve to help us avoid fear, pain and threatening situations. They conserve our energy for more important tasks. Do not label yourself a procrastinator – there is nothing wrong with you. Just be aware that all the little excuses and menial tasks you're doing are a mechanism for self-protection.

3
Why do you procrastinate? You're not sure?

The next time you feel the urge to procrastinate, just put it off.

Have you ever taken months, years or even decades to break up from a partner, only to ask yourself 'why didn't I do that sooner?', once it was all over.

I used to date a girl who was, well, let's call her 'intense'. I fell for her quite quickly, but soon realized our relationship, while it was passionate, wasn't healthy. I had proven reasons not to trust her, but despite this I was still drawn to her. I could not bear the thought of being alone, or anyone else being with her, so I endured the volatility. (You can see I am treading carefully with my words here!) Well after I knew the relationship was 'over', I stayed with her. If she pushed me away, offering me an opening to end it, I'd chase her back. Each time I convinced myself I was going to end it, I just couldn't. I got on really well with her parents and didn't want to upset them. I felt that if it ended things would get messy.

Finally, it all came to a head when she slapped a female friend of mine clean in the face, while she was working in a shop. It all kicked off, and I told her it was over. She didn't accept this and kept turning up at my house. I turned off my phone, and while it was hard for a few days, I got through it. It was quite messy, like I thought it would be, but it didn't last as long as I thought and, after the initial loneliness, I started to feel free and myself again. My friends supported me and took me away while it was still raw to help take my mind off it.

People had been warning me that the relationship wasn't healthy. I knew it, but couldn't accept it. You may not have had this exact experience, but maybe you had children with an ex-partner that made the decision hard? Maybe all your friends were friends you made together? Maybe you felt you were too old or wouldn't get someone as good? Maybe they were there for you in your moment of need and you didn't want to hurt them? Maybe you settled? Maybe you got too comfortable? Maybe you didn't want others to judge you? Maybe you loved them as a friend but the spark was gone? Maybe you feared money would be hard if you broke up?

The guilt and the fear can be strong, but you know the single right decision and action. And you know you know, even if it took hindsight to remind you of what you already knew. You are always stronger and more resourceful than you give yourself credit for. The pain subsides with time. Things *do* get better.

The hard decisions you know you have to make pay dividends long after you make them, but can cause a lot of pain if you delay them. Later in *Start Now. Get Perfect Later*, there is a section dedicated to making bigger and harder decisions.

Remember you are not a procrastinator, but you do sometimes. Often procrastination and indecisiveness aren't as they seem on the surface. There is something hidden behind them. It could be one or more of the following:

☐ Fear of the unknown
☐ Fear of making a mistake or being wrong
☐ Fear of missing out on an alternative
☐ Wanting everything to be perfect or completely ready first

☐ Fear of taking risks
☐ Fear of looking stupid or being judged
☐ Fear of rejection
☐ Fear of being out of your comfort zone
☐ Fear you might not deliver or live up to expectations
☐ Fear of losing or ruining what you already have and have worked hard for
☐ Struggling with clarity or seeing benefits
☐ Waiting for something better to come along
☐ Fear of letting people down or displeasing them
☐ Too many options or overwhelm
☐ It might be right for others, but not for you
☐ Too many people giving you (contrasting) opinions or advice
☐ Doing easy things over important things
☐ The decision or task seems hard, big, or insurmountable
☐ Not sure if you should trust your instincts (you've made mistakes in the past)
☐ You know it intellectually, but still don't do it
☐ Waiting for permission
☐ Second-guessing or doubting yourself
☐ Both or all decisions seem equally hard (part of me this, part of me that)
☐ You will not or are not enjoying it
☐ Frustration (leading to anger or apathy)
☐ You're doing well so you can stop or take a break now
☐ What if this and what if that?
☐ Fear that it is or never will be enough
☐ Fear of success

Maybe you can relate to one or more? These can lead to guilt, frustration, worry, stress or worse. Now before you get overwhelmed and procrastinate on reading the rest of this book, usually all of these can be broken down into:

1 A defence against the fear of failure
2 Indirect resistance to authority
3 A fear of success and the expectations it brings

Procrastination has evolved over time. In our early years the human species existed *because* we procrastinated. Being slow to act saved us from death. Around 100,000 years ago, while *Homo erectus* were busy venturing across continents and the Neanderthals were too cold to venture out of their caves, *Homo sapiens* were engaging in what scientists now call 'complex planning'. This requires us to conceive a future and then plan and determine if a particular action moves us forward. Instead of taking on a mammoth with a spear one-to-one, we took time to conserve our fuel, created the best plan, then threw the spear from a safe distance. Impulsive decision making meant death. A more leisured approach meant life.

Since then, human attitude toward procrastination has evolved with the evolution of value systems. In prehistoric times, it was closely correlated to complex planning and thus led to survival. Today, it is deemed as a failure to complete a task or objective in the form of distraction, overwhelm and putting unimportant easy tasks ahead of bigger, more complex ones. You can see the ongoing conflict between our evolution and today's modern, fast-changing world.

In most cases, indecisiveness and procrastination serve to preserve your self-worth (and survival). But as you will discover, your work is not your worth. You will be armed with modern techniques and thought processes to overwrite your prehistoric survival instinct. These will be explored throughout *Start Now, Get Perfect Later.*

Start Now sound bite

Indecisiveness and procrastination have a deeper, hidden cause and purpose, now outdated, to ensure your survival and preserve your self-worth, and to enable you to avoid pain and fear. Your work is not your worth. You need to use modern techniques to deal with prehistoric programming and embrace the fast-changing world.

4
You are not alone

Whatever your cause of indecisiveness, you are not alone. Every human being has every trait, so what you do, we all do.

When I was an artist, I became a recluse. I worked from home, often through the night. I spent weeks without having much contact with people. I was struggling to sell my work, but didn't have the courage to ask for help. I saw this as a weakness. Having broken free from struggling as an artist, I now realize that asking for help is a sign of courage and strength. Suffering alone, when you are not alone, is unnecessary and keeps you stuck in the problem, rather than seeing a way out.

Anything you have beaten yourself up about, felt guilty or anxious about, we've all done too. The most common ways to procrastinate, according to *Procrastination and the Extended Will* by Joseph Heath and Joel Anderson, are:

- ☐ Checking social media activity
- ☐ Staring at the screen hoping 'work' will go away
- ☐ Cleaning
- ☐ Panicking or taking a nap
- ☐ Working out (or not)
- ☐ Sidetracking on less important tasks/things to do
- ☐ Watching TV and playing video games

I have already done five of these and we're only at Chapter 4 of this book!

It is important to know that procrastination is something we all do, but it doesn't define us. It serves a hidden purpose, but it is not your purpose. Each superficial behaviour of indecisiveness can be seen as just that, an outer behaviour that we all do. If it is seen for what it is, rather than all the self-loathing and inner beatings we give ourselves, we can break the pattern and move on quickly to 'Start Now'.

There are people who brush off indecisiveness, leaving it behind rather than carrying it as baggage; to them it means nothing at all. There are others who wear each act of indecisiveness like an extra layer of clothing, until it becomes so heavy that they are (self-) diagnosed with an illness or disorder. If you avoid being alone, avoid personal responsibility, are easily hurt by criticism or disapproval, have strong fears of abandonment, are very passive or submit in relationships, have difficulty making decisions without support from others, avoid conflict and disagreements and struggle to function socially, you may need to seek professional advice. I am not a doctor, but you are not alone. There are people who can help and want to help. All you have to do is ask.

Start Now sound bite

We all procrastinate. You are not alone. If you are struggling, ask for help. What you are going through, we all are, and there are others who've solved your biggest problem. Asking for help is a sign of strength, not weakness, and often the easiest path to the solution.

5
The hidden benefits of procrastination

Whilst it may seem strange to discuss the benefits of indecisiveness, there are some. Every perceived negative action or emotion has a hidden benefit, or it would not exist. Knowing the hidden purpose of your procrastination helps understand the cause, which in turn helps you solve it faster so you can 'Start Now'.

As discussed already, it saved us from extinction. It conserved energy for life-threatening, highest-value tasks. Procrastination is not a defect or flaw, it is an attempt at coping with attacks on your self-worth. It is a protection against the fear of failure and being judged by others. Historically, this led to being cast of out of society or your tribe, which could result in isolation or death. This is a very good thing to preserve and protect, and a worthy cause of procrastination.

Sometimes procrastination is a preservation of freedom as an indirect resistance to authority. It can be a mechanism to retain control of your life and liberty, which helps you survive and thrive individually and as part of a greater purpose.

Other times indecisiveness protects against a fear of success. Strange to many, but common for others, sabotaging success protects against the weight of expectation, leading to a need to be perceived as perfect, and therefore being judged.

It is rewarding in the moment, an instant fix, to protect our self-worth and relieve pain. This can even be addictive. Sometimes we are rewarded when someone rescues us by doing a task we put off, or when an item of clothing becomes cheaper in a sale later on, or when not facing up to conflict and it being nicer in the moment. We then hope or expect these will happen again and resolve themselves without our actions.

These all link and lead to preservation of your worth and being. The problem these create is their purpose was far more valuable in a more primal society. As humanity, security and technology have developed fast, parts of our brain have not kept pace.

Having a deep understanding of the purpose of indecisiveness helps us to work out how and when it is helping or hindering us. It helps us give it meaning, which stops us from beating ourselves up and allowing it to damage our self-worth. It helps us see it for what it really is, and therefore move on quickly without compounding it further.

It is also a good thing to procrastinate on low-value tasks. Delaying general admin and jobs with no financial or residual benefit, in favour of the most important or highest-value task, is just plain smart. Like preserving energy for a hunt rather than tidying the cave. Procrastinate extra hard in these low-value tasks, and your self- and net worth will increase dramatically.

Start Now sound bite

All methods of indecisiveness serve a greater purpose. Understanding this purpose helps protect us from diminished self-worth, and to contextualize the behaviour as trivial and solvable. Procrastinate hard on low-value tasks that serve as a distraction from important ones.

6

Your work is not your worth

Just like one swallow doesn't make a summer, one fail doesn't make you a failure.

The main reason I failed commercially as an artist, was because I was scared to show (and sell) my work. It's quite hard to sell work that isn't viewed, but I'd convince myself to keep painting in the faint hope that someone would knock on my door and buy all my art and save me from myself.

I now know that creating more art was actually active procrastination to avoid taking my work to galleries, art dealers and entering into competitions. Deep down I knew these were the most important tasks. I had created enough art, and I knew I needed agents, galleries and media to get my work seen and bought. So why did I avoid this and fill my house with new pieces of art that weren't selling just as much as my existing portfolio? Because I was unconsciously protecting my self-worth.

Art was painful for me. For someone to even look at my art, it was like they were critiquing my flawed, naked soul. I couldn't even be in the same room as someone viewing my paintings, in case they didn't like them. I was so sensitive that, unless they gushed over my work, I assumed they hated it but didn't want to tell me. I wouldn't believe them if they said they liked it. I could not separate the identity of me from the critique of my work. I felt like I was being judged; my very being and nature exposed to be chewed up and spat out.

You are not your work, just like I was not my art. My art was an expression of an idea, and your task list is simply a list of actions that get done or don't get done. A job done badly or not at all doesn't define who you are, just like someone critiquing my art doesn't make me a failed human being.

I was so hard on myself. I was my harshest critic of all, but I couldn't see it. I was so protective of my self-worth that I avoided doing anything that could damage it, including basic socializing. The sad irony is the very protection I hid behind was damaging me the most.

Go easy on yourself. Be nice to *you*. You are worth it. You will succeed sometimes, and fail others, but there's no doubt at all that you are amazing, even if your last piece of work was shit! Let your critics be the critics, and you be kind to you.

Start Now sound bite

Have a clear wall of defence between you and your work. The world can judge your work, but that does not define who you are. You are capable of decisiveness, clarity and greatness.

Why do ducks need to be in rows?

There's a saying in Britain that perfectly sums up distraction, procrastination, overwhelm, excuses and lies into one little phrase when it comes to getting things done (or not):

'I'm (just) getting my ducks in a row'.

WTF does that mean anyway?!

Well, there was a fad a little while back where it was popular to put ornamental flying ducks on your wall. Three or four of them in a perfect, ascending line. Beautifully symmetrical and perfect.

Stop. Now.

Trying to get all your ducks in a row is a futile activity, because you can never have all your ducks in a row before you start. Steve Jobs said, 'you can't connect the dots moving forwards, you only can when you're looking backwards'. So much is the irony in this, that getting your ducks in a row has become the very art of procrastination, and a cultural excuse for being busy achieving nothing.

In this section, we will cover all the ways that people (perhaps you) are posturing and pretending and being busy doing nothing, to get all the ducks in a row, before they actually GOYA and JFDI.

7

The pain & paradox of perfection

Perfectionism is often worn as a badge of honour, like it's a trait of greatness. One of the most common answers I see to 'areas of weakness' in a job interview is 'I'm a perfectionist'. They then proceed to spin it into a strength: 'but that makes me sooo great at my job'. Then you hire them. Then six months later they leave because their brain melted out of their ears and they couldn't handle anything being out of place. Screw you for moving one of their ducks.

When I was at university I used to line up all my shirts in colour order from dark to light, with each hanger the exact amount of space apart. I would precisely line up all my Jeffery West boots and tuck them neatly under my shirt rail. I couldn't leave the room until it was perfect. I'd often look as the door was closing, only to rush back in and adjust a hanger or nudge a shoe a nano-inch. I know, I'm weird.

My friends soon cottoned onto this, and started moving the shoes and shirts, just a little at first. They'd watch as I would have to go back and line them all up again. They loved it, and it nearly short-circuited my brain! Whilst I still like tidiness and colour order of clothes today, I don't need a laser measuring device! My kids put my OCD right into perspective and out of the window!

There's a big difference between wanting to be organized and a desire to do something well; and being a pedantic perfectionist. Sure, plan and prepare, but 'Start Now'. Strive for professional and personal excellence, not perfection. It is a curse of progress. The paradox of perfection is that we are perfectly imperfect. Perfect just as we are. We are not broken. We are flawed and unique and we make mistakes. We need to strive for better to grow, to learn and to fight off boredom and atrophy. But the constant pursuit of the unattainable can cause much insecurity, feelings of 'it's never enough', and a paralysis that prolongs the procrastination and pain.

Perfect would be boring anyway. You'd lose purpose. You'd have nowhere else to go and to grow. People are attracted to your flaws (OK, not all of them!). No one relates to perfection.

The pain and paradox of perfection comes from fear, not strength. You might fear the unknown, or making mistakes, or taking risks, or being wrong, or looking stupid, or being judged, or being rejected. You might fear you can't live up to expectations, or letting people down or displeasing them, or that it (or you) is never enough. The decision or task could seem hard; you want to get it just right. You probably weren't perfect the first time you had sex, but that didn't stop you having a go. Ahem.

'Don't wait. The time will never be just right'

Napoleon Hill

Start Now sound bite

Perfectionism can be a curse and a veil to protect your self-worth to avoid the fear of failure and being judged. Strive for excellence instead. 'Start Now. Get Perfect Later'.

23

8

Pre-crastination

It takes a lot of time to do nothing at all.

My Mum loves to tidy up. She will call it a 'clear-out'. I have observed Mum's 'clear-outs' over the years and noticed that she doesn't really 'clear anything out'. She mostly just moves mess and clutter from one place to another place, for a long time. It makes her feel like she's got lots done. I love my Mum, but this is not what you'd call 'deep work'.

Maybe you tidy your desk to get ready for the work ahead? Or the entire house? Maybe you check the news just in case something really important happened in the five minutes since you last checked, that you simply must know about? Be mindful not to delude yourself that you are busy and making progress, when in fact you are putting off the important thing.

Having outed my Mum, I must confess to checking the analytics of my podcast the 'Disruptive Entrepreneur' before I start work. And in each break. Like I'm going to have a million new subscribers just drop in between refreshes. I also check the rankings and number of reviews of my book *Life Leverage*, on Audible (and Amazon). This 'pre-crastination' addiction went into overdrive when the book before this one, *Money* came out. Half of solving the problem is admitting you have one.

Maybe you check Facebook or other social media? Maybe you'll quickly check your emails (again)? Or press the refresh button? Maybe you want to get your ducks in a row? Pre-crastination is 'warming up', but you don't need to 'warm up' to do your most important task, first and fast. So (note to self): stop it. 'Start Now'. Catch yourself out then jump right in to that most important task. Build some momentum. Break the habit and create a new one of getting a good session of work done *first and early*. Reward yourself with some procrastination in your first break. Then faff and posturize and prepare and peacock all you like.

Momentum builds momentum. It takes more energy to start than it does to keep going. The more you 'pre-crastinate' the harder you make it to start. A body in motion tends to stay in motion and a body at rest tends to stay at rest. Don't give yourself a chance to put things off, because it will get harder and harder to start.

Start Now sound bite

Pre-crastination is the illusion of busyness we create by 'getting things ready' before we start. Catch yourself out. Save your faffing, checking and moving things from one place to another for your first break, where you can reward yourself with some procrastination. 'Start Now'.

9
Active procrastination

Who's the easiest person to lie to? You got it. You. A relative of 'pre-crastination' is 'active procrastination'. Also known as the busy fool. Like a lemming who walks a lot but without knowing where they are going only to be led to a cliff to walk off.

There are two forms of 'active procrastination':

1 Have you ever got to the end of your very busy day, having been dragged from pillar to post by everyone else, helping them solve their problems at the expense of your own, dealing with other people's emergencies that they make yours, only to realize you got very little meaningful work done?

2 Have you ever convinced yourself at the end of your mad-rush day that you were very busy, ticking low priority things off your list regularly, putting off the big things, only to realize you got very little meaningful work done?

Point 1 is 'active procrastination' through others. Allowing others to dictate the flow and productivity of your time and tasks. You might achieve results for others, but not for you. You may do this because you are paid to, because you find it hard to say no, or because you have no focus or prioritization of your own.

Point 2 is 'active procrastination' by deluding yourself that you're busy, when all you are doing is the mundane very well, and the important badly or, worse, not at all.

Active procrastination is delusion. It is like an alter ego, taunting you in your mind, manipulating you into doing things the real you knows you shouldn't be doing. But you can't help it. It mocks you. It feeds off you. It is often your biggest killer of progress and productivity. It is smart and devious. It is convincing at having you believe you're busy. 'Go on, you know you don't want to. Do it later, be-yatch.' This has a persona. I call it my inner bas-tard. Chapter 54 is dedicated to 'it'.

You have to take control of this sadistic version of you. Catch yourself making yourself busy for no good reason other than to feel good, and break the pattern. Immediately 'Start Now' at something important and high up on your priority list. Address an important decision. Do deep and meaningful work. Defeat the gremlins.

My wife is always busy. I'm sure you know someone like that. I wanted her to be less busy, for altruistic reasons of course, and she has asked me not to make any sexual references in my books anymore. So I paid for a cleaner, a cook, a gardener, an extra PA to help with home and personal work, a driver, an au pair, we have grandparents for babysitting, and I'm still not getting any more sex.

Start Now sound bite

Beware of 'active procrastination': being busy for the sake of feeling busy. It's like eating a tub of Ben & Jerry's: it feels good at the time but the guilt kicks in later. Catch yourself out, break the pattern, and do a high-value task or make an important decision now.

10
'Don't put off until tomorrow…

…what you can do the day after tomorrow just as well'

Mark Twain

Have you seen the film *Withnail and I?* The student protagonists lived in squalor, never cleaning or washing up. This is how my fellow students and I treated our shared kitchens at university. I shared the downstairs kitchen with Mike, and the way we cleaned the crockery and cutlery was to throw them away and buy new ones. As this was costing money, we gave up throwing them away and simply stacked the kitchen sink and surrounds higher and higher and higher with dirty pans and plates. In the end it got so overfull that we locked the door and left it to rot.

I think we both hid the kitchen away in a dark compartment in our minds so deep we convinced ourselves it didn't exist. Another term would go by, and the door was still locked. Occasionally I'd walk past, imagine that I could hear something, and dive quickly into my room. We stayed in the same house from our second to third years. This was very convenient, as we didn't have to clean the kitchen out. We used Kev and Trigger's kitchen, which they were unhappy about, and had regular take-aways. Terms drifted by again, until the last day of the last year of our degree, when the task we'd been avoiding for nearly two years reared its ugly head.

Mike and I did not want to undertake this task. I think I asked (made) Mike to go in first. He slowly unlocked the door, inched it open, and thousands of flies flew out in a tornado-like swarm, completely filling the entire ground floor of the house. They were like mutant bluebottles: fat, hungry and angry. We waded and fought through them. The stench was indescribably putrid, with vile mould and rot everywhere.

It took us a full day to fumigate that kitchen. We had to throw most of the kitchenware away. We scrubbed and scrubbed and scrubbed the hardware. It was a humiliating, humbling experience that our other student mates enjoyed immensely.

When you put things off, they rot and rot until they stink. A decision to do nothing, to put it off, to bury your head in the sand, is still a decision. It does *not* go away. No one comes and cleans your kitchen for you. It gets bigger and bigger and worse and worse until something gives. You can have a lingering hope that someone will save you, but risk takers and change makers do not take this view. Do. Not. Bury. Your Head. In. The. Sand. Do not hide away from the truth you can hear in your head. Do not kid yourself it can wait. You know what you have to do, so get on and *do it now*.

Once we had cleaned the kitchen I felt free and liberated. It was like a two-year weight had been lifted off my shoulders. Like being released from a prison. And that is how you will feel when you get important, hard tasks done first and fast.

Start Now sound bite

Do not put off until tomorrow what needs to be done today. 'Start Now'. Do. Not. Delay. A decision to do nothing is still a decision, and that all-important task will get nastier and bigger and hairier until you sort it out. Take a deep breath. Do not think. Just 'Start Now'.

11
Task jumping

How many browsers do you have open on your computer at any one time? How many websites or apps on your phone? How many unfinished tasks or started-but-never-finished actions? If the answer is more than one or two, it is likely you're task jumping. It is often the illusion of progress manifested in the delusion of busyness.

Another easy lie we can tell ourselves is that we are 'multi-tasking'. We feel we can take on more than one job at a time. We like the variety of having different things to do. Some people even tell us we are good at multi-tasking or, worse, we have convinced ourselves that we are. Some of us even get a buzz from it. But the only task jump that we make should be a break.

The only multi-task should be something you can do passively, that doesn't need your conscious attention, along with something that you do actively. A podcast while in the gym is legitimate, effective multi-tasking. Texting someone in a meeting is not. Working on your book while on a plane to the Bahamas is legitimate, effective multi-tasking. Looking on Facebook while on a date is not.

Task jumping is a behaviour. Whilst the first task jump might seem innocuous enough, you then jump from the new task to a newer one, and onto a newer one, and so on and on and on. Before you know it, you have lots of things started and nothing finished. Like a computer that has so many browsers open it grinds to a halt, you get frazzled and your memory doesn't work as fast. Then you overheat!

Each time you jump from task to task you get out of your flow state, where you had momentum; where you are IN the task, with the least resistance. You might call this being in the 'zone' or the 'groove'. It takes time to get into this state. Remember a body in motion tends to stay in motion, and a body at rest tends to stay at rest. Shockingly, according to Gloria Mark's *The Cost of Interrupted Work: More Speed and Stress*, it takes an average of 23 minutes and 15 seconds to get back to the task. WTF? You could have done the entire damn task in the time it took to jump out and in again!

Mihaly Csikszentmihalyi, author of *Flow*, calls the flow state 'an optimal state of intrinsic motivation, where the person is fully immersed in what they are doing'. You know that feeling, where time stands still or disappears because you were so into what you were doing. Once you are in that state, let the momentum carry you along and stay in it for as long as you have the energy. Later in *Start Now. Get Perfect Later*, I'll share a simple technique: a system you can follow, that helped me stay focused to write this book and get other major tasks done, that you can use too.

According to Gloria Mark, a Professor at the University of California: 'People switched activities on average of every three minutes and five seconds... people not only switched between small tasks, but also between entire projects every 10 and half minutes'. WTAF?! If you task jump just five times a day, that could be up to two hours spent jumping between just 15 minutes spent on the actual small tasks, and less than one hour on important projects. Imagine how much of your life you will liberate if you stay on task.

My small, male, linear brain hates being interrupted. In a second I can so easily forget what I was just doing or thinking. And then I worry that what I'd forgotten so fast was very important. And then I get frustrated with the interrupter. And then I bark at the interrupter. And then I forget why. And then as the interrupter is usually my wife, I have to apologize. And then I know I will receive my due punishment later that night. Or not, as is usually the case. I'm sure I'm not the only one, right? Right?

There will always be something that someone else perceives as urgent, to stop you from the important thing you are doing, right now. And as long as you allow that to happen, the important will not get done and everything will become urgent and you will go from fire to fire reactively trying to solve issues that you could and should have prioritized weeks ago. So stop allowing it to happen. Stop spraying your energy all over the place, wasting and misplacing most of it. Simple tips to stop yourself doing this are in upcoming chapters.

People task jump in their careers and lifestyles too. They fail to commit to the most important thing, and try a few side businesses, feeling they can juggle and progress with them all. Often, they fear missing out (FOMO) on a great opportunity. But as soon as it gets hard, or doesn't meet their (unrealistic) expectations, they change, under the delusion that it will be easier or better next time around. And they repeat this pattern their entire lives. Many people do this with dating and relationships, hedging their bets and having multiple 'back-up plans', only to not fully focus on plan (person) A. After all, you don't need a plan B if you make plan A work. They play snakes and ladders with their work and their private lives, stopping and starting and chopping and changing again and again, all over again.

So, go narrow and deep, not shallow and wide. And a huge added bonus of focused, single-task-oriented deep work without task jumping is this, according to Mihaly (because his first name is way easier) in *Flow*:

'The best moments in our lives are not the passive, receptive, relaxing times…The best moments usually occur if a person's body or mind is stretched to its limits in a voluntary effort to accomplish something difficult and worthwhile. In this (flow) state they are completely absorbed in an activity, especially an activity which involves their creative abilities. During this 'optimal experience' they feel strong, alert, in effortless control, unselfconscious, and at the peak of their abilities.'

(And I only jumped three times in this chapter and now feel a deep sense of fulfilment for finishing it. I think I'll take a break!)

Start Now sound bite

Task jumping is NOT multi-tasking, it is time wasting. It can take between 2× and 8× more time to complete a task if you jump and flit between too many tasks. The time (void) between tasks consumes the most energy, as a body in motion tends to stay in motion. All the energy is in the starting again, again. Turn off all distractions, isolate yourself and maintain your flow state for as long as you can. Some simple tools to do this are in forthcoming chapters.

12
The myth of BIG decisions

People think decisions take years; they don't. People think decisions are huge; they're not. People think decisions are single events; they rarely are.

A single decision takes a split-nanosecond. It's just all the leading up to that decision that takes all the time and energy. It's the noise and doubts and fears and second-guessing yourself, and the voices and the thought of how others will judge you, that cloud or drag out the single, split-decision. All the things in your head that took days, weeks or even years, were just preparation for the decision, and much of it is unnecessary distraction.

A single decision is small. It is a single, unique thought; a tiny spec of energy in your brain. And then it's gone, replaced by the next. It is estimated that an adult makes about 35,000 remotely conscious decisions each day (in contrast a child makes about 3,000). This number may sound absurd but, in fact, we make 226.7 decisions each day on just food alone, according to researchers at Cornell University (Wansink and Sobal, 2007). And according to Tony Ablewhite of the Puzzler Mind Gym, the average person makes 773,618 decisions in a lifetime, but lives to regret as many as 143,262 of them. You can't make this many big decisions in your life, your brain would melt out of your eye holes.

A single decision isn't really a single decision. What you perceive as a single or big decision, is actually a build-up of many small preceding decisions. If you've been in a relationship break up, you don't go from 'in love' to 'over' in a nanosecond. There are months or years of smaller questions and decisions that compound towards what you perceive to be a big, single decision. But all the ones before it already made that decision. Even if you find out, out of the blue, that you've been cheated on, there are still many decisions that come between 'happy' and 'over'. In fact, many people decide to stay in the relationship, *but* they need to keep re-making that decision daily. Others make the decision, only to go back on it months or years later.

People put so much weight on single decisions like they are bigger than they really are; that they are the be-all and end-all of life. It doesn't help you to make smarter, faster and bigger decisions if you give them more weight and size than they really have. Think BIG but start small.

Success is not a single decision. It is a decision to 'Start Now. Get Perfect Later'. Once that decision is made, which is quick and easy, (only) *then* a series of decisions along the journey are sparked off. Some of those decisions are good ones that build on good ones, and others are bad ones that set you back a little. Keep deciding forward. Sometimes you just need to fail forward fast. Diminish the weight of importance of big decisions by chunking down to each small-step decision.

The 'eureka' moment so often seen in films of that revelatory moment of inspiration and genius, in the bath or shower, is mostly good story telling and fodder for media. Most people, even the ones we hold in the highest regard in society, don't have single 'eureka' moments. They make hundreds or thousands of decisions that build into this perceived single breakthrough idea, like the apparent overnight success that took 10 years to build. They often iterate thousands of actions to work towards an epiphany, like the 10,000 experiments Edison undertook before finally getting his 'lightbulb'. Let it be said that there are no big decisions. If you're stuck or overwhelmed, decide your way out of it, small decision by small decision.

Start Now sound bite

Most big decisions are made up of lots of much smaller decisions. Decisions take split-nanoseconds to make but can take years to prepare for. Reduce the weight and size of decisions by breaking them down, knowing you will make lots of good (small) ones and a few bad (small) ones, along your journey to success. So start making more (small) decisions.

13

What you worry about rarely comes about

Have you ever had an argument with someone…

…in your head?!

Ha! Sure you have. Someone said something to you, or wrote a curt email, or cut you up in the car, or just gave you a little look, and off you went inside your own head having a great big argument. Maybe you unleashed the fury on them? Maybe you imagined them having a pop right back at you? Ding dong ding dong for hours or days at a time. I once was so preoccupied with having a heated debate with someone in my head, at an event I was the main speaker at, that I walked right down the long corridor and into the toilets and followed someone virtually into the cubicle with my flies almost undone before I realized it was the ladies.

These arguments in your head can even be with people you've never met before. You have no actual idea of what they would say in real life. These inner arguments can consume your imagined life and disrupt your real life. And then it doesn't actually happen at all, in the real world. Or at least doesn't play out anything like the movie in your mind.

And so it is with being indecisive, or getting started, or overwhelm. All those fears and doubts and the weight of big decisions that stop you from taking the first step are (mostly) illusions. How people will judge you, the past mistakes you made and the unknown future are all illusions, because events are uniquely different each time.

37

Worry is simply an imagined future that has a very high chance of being wrong, that can significantly affect or ruin the here and now.

You don't know how it will be, so stop imagining all of the terrible scenarios. As you can hopefully now see, all those things you think that might happen that you create in your head rarely, if ever, do. The reality is mostly different and unique, so screw it and just do it. Or at least start it. Let the reality be as it will be.

And even if you do make a bad decision, you can make it right with your next, small decision. Later in *Start Now. Get Perfect Later* you'll learn how to stop dwelling on the past, cover off your imagined worst-case scenarios, remove perceived decision-permanence and contextualize your imagined fears and tough decisions. If presidents can make decisions knowing people will die from them, then you can start writing your book, or pick up the phone and have a hard conversation, or whatever else you know you need to do but have been putting off.

Start Now sound bite

What you worry about rarely comes about, like an argument in your own head. Almost every time your worry doesn't play out as you feared, so stop living in the past or future. Make a decision and let it be, knowing you can change course at any time to control the outcome.

14
Don't dwell on the past…

I have an ex-girlfriend (same one; I'm no stud), who had an ex-boyfriend. Let's call him 'Dick'. My ex-girlfriend would frequently say to me, 'Dick used to do that, I don't like it. Stop it. Don't be like Dick.' Then she'd say, 'Why won't you do this, that and the other, like Dick used to?'

'Well why don't you piss off back to Dick then?'

I never said it, I just thought it. I was a wimp. I don't know what Dick did to her, but he sure made a sizeable, lasting impression.

Living in the past, whether it's by comparison to how it used to be, the inability to let go and move on, nostalgia, guilt, embarrassment, shame or resentment, is a sure way not to move forward. And it can take years to stay in the same place, or even go backwards. Funny how it can take so long to get nowhere. Or not funny.

The past is the past. It's done. It cannot be changed, but the memory and meaning of it, and how it is shaping your future, can be. The quicker you move on, the better your life will be. The past does not have to dictate the future, yet it does for many. Those strong emotions manifesting in the inability to forgive others (or themselves) for past perceived mistakes, only really damages one person: them (you).

You wouldn't pick up a polar bear, put him on your back and carry him around with you everywhere you go: a 50-year piggy back. Yet people are carrying their emotional baggage around with them their whole life, weighing them down more and more like a big hairy animal. The longer you do it, the heavier it gets. And then it starts making demands: 'Oi Rob, I'm hungry. Get me food now. Oi Rob, I'm thirsty, take me for a drink. Oi Rob, I need to go to the toilet.' And then it starts to rule your life. And then it affects your interaction with others. 'Rob, why have you brought that polar bear out on our date?' 'Oh, didn't I tell you on my Tinder profile? I take him everywhere I go. I have been for decades. OK, I'll get my coat.'

I reconnected with an old school friend, Dave, recently. It was great to see him, and he seemed to be in a good place in his life. He knew me when I was very overweight, and as we went down the memory lane of nearly 30 years, I raised things that happened (like swimming class in my Speedos and PE in my Y-fronts; sorry to do that to you) that he had no recollection of at all. There's me, still emotionally scarred nearly three decades on, and he didn't even remember, because he didn't care. Like all the things we think we are being judged on, people are too busy thinking or worrying about their own lives and problems to remember, like yesterday, a 10-year-old Rob with his Y-fronts pulled up to his armpits. Don't be like Rob. Be like Dave.

The past does not dictate the future, so don't allow it to. Only you can stop that happening by seeing that today is a new day, and it won't be the same as tomorrow. It will bring both new opportunities and new challenges. Your new date is not like your ex, so don't ruin it before you start. Your new employee or boss are not like your old ones, they are unique individuals with different strengths and weaknesses. Realize that if they do or say something that picks at your past emotions, it is your recall and link to these memories, and not the current situation, that's playing out.

According to research at Northwestern University (Donna Bridge, Feinberg School of Medicine), your memory of an event is not actually a memory of the event, but a recall (memory) of the last recall (memory) of the event. The more recalls, the more the memory changes, like Chinese whispers. So, you can be holding on to events that have changed over time and become even further from the past reality. And that's kind of nuts.

Start Now sound bite

Live in the moment. Allow it to play out with curiosity, and don't ruin it by bringing your baggage into the present. Let go. Forgive yourself and others. Don't dwell on the past...fail forward fast.

15
What other people think of you…

…should have no bearing on your decisions, unless it is a moral or ethical judgement call or action. If you spend your life making decisions reacting and second-guessing what other people think of you, that's a guaranteed way to never be authentic to who you really are. And to be really busy dealing with other people's problems and putting off your own.

And what other people think of you…

…is none of your business anyway.

…and they're too preoccupied with their own life to be thinking about how you're thinking about how they're thinking about you.

I went on my first public speaking course in Australia in 2006. It was a life-changing week, where I felt very challenged and vulnerable, but grew into loving getting my message out to the world and inspiring people. I remember being so worried about what my fellow would-be speakers were thinking of my terrible attempts at presenting. It consumed me.

I went on to design and deliver public speaking courses once my skills and experience were at the right level. Over and over and over I see people feeling the same vulnerable feelings like I did. Some people even break down in tears. I now realize this is silly, because when you are doing your speaking exercises on my speaking course, your fellow speakers, acting as the audience for your speech, aren't even listening to you at all. They are too busy shitting themselves about being up next! Most of the things you think people are watching and judging you on, are the same fear that the speaker up next has. They're too consumed with themselves to care (or even notice) what you're doing.

We spend on average 1 hour 50 minutes a day fretting, amounting to 12 hours 53 minutes a week – or 4 years 11 months across the average adult lifetime of 64 years. All that time wasted worrying about things that won't happen and people thinking things about you that they're not thinking. And most of them don't appreciate what you do anyway. As Churchill said: 'You will never reach your destination if you stop and throw stones at every dog that barks'. You want more time in your life? Just halving your worry of what others might be thinking of you will free two years' worth of thoughts!

Making or delaying decisions based on what others think of you is a sure-fire way to stay frustrated, live someone else's vision and negate your own happiness. It's also illogical. You know what is best for you; others do not. You live your life and the consequences of your decisions; others do not. Making decisions to please others or to avoid their criticism or judgement is like saving money in someone else's bank account.

People pleasing, a strong need to be liked or loved, fear of judgement or ridicule by others, all have the primal purpose of avoiding tribal exile. But this is not the beginnings of human civilization anymore. Your primitive brain may not have caught up, but your conscious mind and decision-making faculties can.

People will judge you anyway. The very first car I had was a mostly rusty, white Vauxhall Astra. I wanted to improve it so people wouldn't judge me, so I had it lowered. I put a big bore exhaust on it, and a K&N upgraded air filter. When I used to drive around McDonald's car park, some people used to call me a 'wankaaa'. When I became a millionaire by 31, I bought my first Ferrari, the 430 Spider. Surely people would love me now. When I used to drive down Peterborough high street, some people used to call me a 'wankaaa'.

If people will judge you anyway, then you might as drive the car you want. If people will judge you anyway, you might as well make decisions that are right for you and those you care about. When you remove the worries and second-guesses of how others perceive you, you have fewer variables in your decision-making process, resulting in less overwhelm and ultimately more clarity. Be yourself. You're the very best at being you, and everyone else is taken. When you are true to yourself, you attract the right people who accept and like you for who you are.

Some people will hate about you they very thing that is great about you.

Start Now sound bite

Worrying about what other people think about you is time consuming, draining and distracting. People will judge you no matter what you decide or do, so do the thing that is best for yourself and those you care about. Be yourself and you will find those who like you for who you are, not who you are pretending to be.

16
The void & the unknown

All good decisions, bad decisions and non-decisions are a step into the unknown. Many people delay decisions because they want to know all the facts or variables up front. This is an impossible position. Others fear the unknown. Yet everything we will ever decide is a step into the unknown. Even procrastinating is a step into the unknown, as you don't know what will happen when you put off a decision. Putting off a decision because the future is unknown often becomes the worst decision.

This might sound like common sense but, because each and every possible scenario of the future is unknown, you might as well make a (proactive, imperfect, not-quite-ready) decision. It's an illusion that you're safer delaying or not making a decision, because that has as many unknowns as a positive decision.

The point where procrastination sits I call the 'void'. The void is the black hole mid-point between a good decision and a bad decision. It is in a vacuum of non-decision, yet ironically it is still a decision. The good decision is unknown, the bad decision is unknown, but the illusion is that the void is known and comfortable. In this void, you feel safe for a while. Then guilt and worry set in and you experience a long, slow, not-quite-painful-enough-to-do-anything-decisive pain.

You fear making a decision because of a perceived sharp pain, despite the fact that a good decision could give you much pleasure. So, you stay in the void like the frog that stays in the water that ever-so-slowly increases in temperature, only to boil to death as the heat that it didn't notice caught up with it.

Sure, you may make a wrong decision. We all make wrong decisions. But you did your best at the time. You will have decided forward. You can correct a wrong decision fast. This turns a perceived wrong decision into a right one, so it could be argued that it was in fact part of the right decision. You'll recall that there are no big decisions, just a series of smaller ones, and some of those will be 'wrong' ones. Every great decision contained wrong decisions in it, all rolled up.

No decision keeps you in the void of nothingness. No decision is not the same as a decision to wait. Know the difference. But don't kid yourself that no decision is a proactive step forward. People can live in the void for decades, only to look back with deep regret that they should have set up their own business sooner or married that person (or divorced that person), or spent more time with their kids.

Every non-decision is still a decision not to do anything, which keeps you stuck in the void. Habits form slowly but are then hard to shake off. Deciding becomes a habit, as does staying in the void. Exercise it like a muscle. 'Start Now. Get Perfect Later'.

Start Now sound bite

All decisions — good, bad and nothing — are unknowns. Don't waste your life stuck in the void of non-decision, fearing the unknown, as all is unknown. There are good and bad decisions in all good decisions. A bad decision may give you a short sharp pain, but the void of non-decisions will give you a slow, creep-up-on-you ache for a lifetime.

17
Part of me this, part of me that

Have you ever felt that 'part of you' wanted something, but 'part of you' didn't? Or wanted to do something else? Or that you knew how to do something, but weren't doing it? That could be eating well, going to the gym, leaving your job to set up your own business, or becoming more disciplined around money. It could be that something holds you back from letting yourself earn a fortune, or making an important decision (or any decision).

I feel the reason for this is natural balance. We experience a natural order that is balanced by polar opposites that exist all around us. Every human being experiences these polar opposites: love and hate, fear and confidence, narcissism and altruism, control and chaos, and so on.

In every decision you have to make at any time, you could potentially experience each polar opposite, often simultaneously. There's a cost and a consequence to every decision; good or bad, bad or good. You can't have upside without downside, or loss without benefit, and so sometimes you get stuck procrastinating in the void. Then you feel frustrated. Or overwhelmed. Or, worse, paralysed. The easiest thing to do at this time is nothing, or keep doing what you're already doing, and so nothing changes. This pull of 'part of me this, part of me that' can then damage your confidence and self-worth.

You want to start a new business but it's risky and you have expenses. You're unhappy in a relationship but you don't want to be alone. You want to make boat loads of cash but you don't want to be seen to be greedy or commercial. These 'part of me this, part of me that' feelings are the natural, omnipresent polarized possibilities in any situation. This does not mean that YOU are indecisive, or that you procrastinate, or even that you can't do it. This only means what it is: that you are experiencing all polarized parts of your decision, existent in any and all decisions.

I'm often told by people I help that they 'know what to do but aren't doing it'. They too are experiencing polarized emotions that splits them into their perceived 'parts'. The trouble with 'part of me this, part of me that' is that it makes decisions harder, longer and less clear. It damages self-worth because time wasted or stuck creates regret, remorse or comparison to others. You spend your thoughts looking at the downside of what you didn't do, rather than the upside of what you should do.

I see these polarized, 'part of me this, part of me that' feelings as feedback. You are being shown all extremes of any decision, giving you the innate ability to weigh up both the upsides and downsides; to evaluate the risk and the reward, and then make an informed decision. It is naive to think that any decision is all good or all bad. None is, no matter how extreme you might think it is. Seeing both (or all) sides simultaneously can be polarizing, but it also gives you more balanced, holistic information to evaluate each decision with wisdom. There's nothing wrong with you if you're torn, you're just experiencing paradoxical balance.

Allow yourself a little time to be torn; it is good feedback that it's an important decision and that you are evaluating all sides. Then commit to making your decision, taking into account all you've learned so far. If you are still stuck...

...get off the fence, all it does is hurt your arse.

Start Now sound bite

Being torn in a state of 'part of me this, part of me that' is natural. This polarization can create confusion, but it also gives you clarity as you are able to see all options. When feeling torn, allow yourself to see all sides and then make a proactive decision, knowing you have more wisdom than only seeing one side.

18
What if you don't decide to decide? Part 1.

What won't you achieve?
Where will you not go?
What might you regret?
Who will you not love?
Who might you not become?
What will you not leave behind?

These are all questions that could remain unanswered, that you may have to live with the rest of your life, if you don't start making some decisions fast. Part 2 of this short chapter (Chapter 63) will go into what those unanswered questions and regrets are, so you don't have to live with them. It is wise to think of the painful consequences of *not* deciding, to balance all the thoughts you mull over about what you *are* deciding.

So let's move to the next section and give you some simple tools to banish overwhelm and 'Start Now'.

SECTION 3

Banish overwhelm & Start Now

19
There are no bad decisions

Of course, looking back, there are apparent (big) bad decisions you feel you've made. Decisions that you wouldn't make again, with hindsight. But therein lies the paradox. You will make a better decision in the future *because* of the perceived (big) bad decision you made in the past. This has helped you make a better decision now. One apparent bad decision led to and created a better one. And so it compounds onwards and upwards.

Even if you struggle to see it that way, and you really regret a bad decision, holding onto that regret (other than as motivation) doesn't serve you. It will keep you in the past, thus affecting your present and future. You are best letting it go and moving on. Even if at first you have to try to kid yourself, a bad decision seen as a bad decision only holds you back from moving forward.

Whatever way you look at it, a bad decision is, and must be seen to be, a good decision for your own progress and sanity. If you perceive you made a bad decision, you may beat yourself up about it, hold on to it, and remain in the past with it. But for a bad outcome to come about, no one big bad decision but a string of smaller decisions would have lead to that point. Which means you can make smaller decisions to get out of the situation as easily as you got into it.

People don't get into huge debt with a single big bad decision. They perform a series of very small, routine purchases on credit, and over time it builds and compounds. It is the same for buying coffees and lunches out that only cost a few pounds a day but become a habit and build up to thousands a year. Get a few Ubers instead of the underground, have just a couple of drinks a few times a week, open up your emails or social media when you are trying to do deep work; these all eventually lead to bigger problems, but take time and slowly creep up on you.

You make the best decisions you can, with the knowledge, experience and resources you have available to you at the time. You never intentionally make bad decisions, so be kind to yourself and accept that you are doing your best. If you want to make better decisions, get better information and resources (and learn from each perceived bad decision to compound your experience).

Most decisions are not final anyway. You can always make another forward decision, a better decision, or even a U-turn decision. Stop thinking that every decision you make is about life or death. If you make a wrong decision, you can right it fast. Bad decisions can be made good quicker than you may think.

You don't learn as much from good decisions, so good decisions aren't as good as you think. Therefore, bad decisions are better than you think, because of what you learn and carry forward from them. As long as you see this balance, then you can get better at making good decisions.

Start Now sound bite

There are no single bad decisions, just lots of small decisions. There are great lessons to be learned from decisions you perceive to be bad, and these will help you get better at making good decisions. Even if a decision was a disaster, holding onto that only makes it worse. Even if you have to kid yourself at first, see every decision as a good one and it becomes one.

20

Overwhelm me, I love it

'If you want something done, ask a busy person'

Benjamin Franklin

Whilst overwhelm can of course lead to procrastination, rabbit in the headlights and head in the sand, slightly too much to do can also encourage great people to achieve great things. That includes you.

Steve Jobs was famous for his 'reality distortion field' (RDF). According to Wikipedia, it was his 'ability to convince himself and others to believe almost anything…RDF was said to distort an audience's sense of proportion and scales of difficulties and made them believe that the task at hand was possible'.

Many people are looking to reduce overwhelm and are, ironically, doing nothing, because they have the 'paradox of choice'. Yet with not quite enough to do, less or nothing gets done because there's no motivation, no 'to do' list to get through or no challenging deadline to hit.

This is my 10th book. When I get focused and write deeply, I can get a book thrashed out in between two and four weeks, realistically. But sometimes it takes me three to nine months to do two to four weeks writing. This is always when I don't have much on, I don't have an imposed deadline, or I don't have a strong need or urgency. Sometimes I have to impose that on myself, to game myself into action. And sometimes you have to second-guess yourself, knowing that you will let yourself off the hook unless you get serious.

My first stint at writing this book got me about one third through. It was going well, and pretty easy, so I relaxed. Without meaning to, I had three months off. After discussions with my publisher, and a target month to launch the book, this focused my mind to starting again. But as it can take many months to go from final manuscript to book release, I found something else to do each day, knowing that if I 'start tomorrow' I'll still have time. In the end, I said 'enough is enough' to myself, and put out a request in my 'Disruptive Entrepreneur' (Facebook) community. I offered to pay for 10 people's travel and accommodation to have a private read and critique of the book, to help me get a better edit. I set a challenging date for two weeks' time, knowing I'd have to get prolific, *and* I had other commitments.

This did of course help to produce a book that has been scrutinized before release, but even more critical was the hard deadline that now couldn't be missed under any circumstances. Wasting all that money and letting those people down was a strong motivator that really focused the mind. It upped my chapter per day ratio from one or two at best, to five or more.

At this time, I had six full public speaking days and two courses to run. I hadn't had this many in the whole of the year and, bang, here they are when I had two weeks to finish a book. Despite having slightly too much on, I completed all the speaking days and courses, hitting my five chapter a day target, and managed to get good golf time in with Bobby and binge watch some Netflix with my wife. If you are reading this, it means I made it happen. And please don't think I am some kind of Arnie. I put things off to stay comfortable and avoid hard things just as much as anyone else. There will be more techniques like this in Chapter 34.

Don't be too scared of overwhelm. Give yourself and others you manage ever-so-slightly too much to do, trust yourself and those around you to get it done, set imposed deadlines to focus the mind, and get stuck in.

Of course, 935 plates spinning at once will melt your brain. Avoid the following scenarios to keep your overwhelm at the 'just slightly too much' level, and not the 'holy-shit-fuck' level:

- ☐ Don't take the advice or listen to the opinions of too many people or leaders
- ☐ Don't say yes to every opportunity that comes your way
- ☐ Don't have too many apps or browsers open at any one time
- ☐ Don't give yourself too many choices, even in social or mundane situations
- ☐ Don't have unrealistic expectations that you can do everything yourself
- ☐ Don't feel you need to have all your ducks in a row before you start
- ☐ When you are in flow, do not allow yourself to be interrupted until a break

Embrace the paradox of overwhelm by avoiding the above, but embracing the buzz, energy and great feeling you get by ticking things off your list and by having your own RDF with yourself and others you lead or manage. As you do this, you will build your decision muscle to be able to take on and achieve more and more, with the same apparent effort, or even less.

But just as important as managing being busy is when you take a break. Whether it is for 15 minutes or four weeks, make sure you take it. After an intense work period, you will need this recovery time to remain prolific and avoid burn-out.

Start Now sound bite

Steve Jobs was famous for his reality distortion field (RDF) that pushed himself and those around him to not only get more done, but achieve things they thought previously impossible. Embrace the paradox of overwhelm by giving yourself and others just a little too much to do, as opposed to not enough. Then impose deadlines and strong reasons to hit those challenging targets.

21

The paradox of choice

Professor Barry Schwartz demonstrated in the *Paradox of Choice: Why More Is Less*, that having too many things to choose from often leads to the consumer feeling bewildered when facing the choice, and less satisfied even after taking a decision. He cites studies that indicate people are less likely to buy a product when faced with too many choices.

Researchers set up two displays of jams at a gourmet food store for customers to try samples, who were given a coupon for a dollar off if they bought a jar. In one display there were six jams, in the other 24: Of the people exposed to the smaller selection, 30% bought a jam, but only 3% of those exposed to the larger selection did.

Another example cited is that of 401k savings plans. The more fund choices offered by employers offering matching 401k plans, the fewer people actually selected any fund at all, even though that meant foregoing 'free' money.

As the number of choices increases, it peaks and people tend to feel more pressure, confusion and, potentially, dissatisfaction; which in turn hinders their practical thinking. Too many options are mentally draining and create 'noise' in the brain, leading to irrational choices. In moments of being overwhelmed, such as having many tasks to do or a particularly difficult one, there is a fight (resistance) or flight (ignore) reaction, which can include fear and anxiety. That's useful if we are being hunted, but not as key when we are making a difficult phone call or writing a chapter of a book.

I see both the irony and paradox in this chapter coming right after 'Overwhelm me, I love it', but this is exactly what we are all trying to balance: not enough to motivate us to do something, and too much to overwhelm us to do nothing.

In many areas of your life, both the seemingly important and apparently mundane, you will need to reduce the choices to increase the ease of decision and action. Steve Jobs always wore his now famous black turtle neck, jeans and trainers not just for brand repetition, but to reduce 'decision fatigue'. Someone in the position of Steve Jobs would likely have to make many very important and big decisions in a day. The last thing he needs is to get overwhelmed on what to wear. Simon Cowell is the same. Whilst this can seem like a small thing, with the number of decisions we have to make each day, the last thing we need is 117 options each time.

In research by Jonathan Levav of Stanford and Shai Danziger of Ben-Gurion University, three prisoners had completed at least two-thirds of their sentences, but the parole board granted freedom to only one of them. The cases were heard at 8:50am, 3.10pm and 4.25pm. There was a pattern to the parole board's decisions. It was all about timing, as researchers discovered by analysing more than 1,100 decisions over the course of a year. Prisoners who appeared early in the morning received parole about 70% of the time, while those who appeared late in the day were paroled less than 10% of the time. The odds favoured the prisoner who appeared at 8:50am, and he did in fact receive parole. They were just asking for parole at the wrong time of day, because the parole board were more tired and decision fatigued later in the day. More on the timing of decision fatigue later.

My beautiful, loving, smart, amazing wife and I used to go out for dinner a couple of times a week, back in the day. Obviously, this was before we had kids, and when we might have had what could be perceived as a 'life'. Each time we would spend half an hour or more debating which restaurant to go to. Despite there only being half a dozen decent ones in Peterborough, it would take us ages. And most of the time, we'd end up agreeing to go back to our favourite, Jim's Bistro.

Sometimes when I 'retire' for the evening, laying in bed in the distant hope that my wife will join me under the duvet for a 'cuddle' before I nod off, I'll have a quick search on Netflix for the next documentary to watch. Sometimes I can spend an hour scrolling and watching trailers, never to actually choose an episode. Even when I go to my favourites to force myself into a decision, there are about 14,000 shows I've 'favourited' and so my brain overheats. Then I fall asleep. Then I miss my wife joining me in bed. This repeats itself! Don't be like Rob.

These are, of course, First World problems. Please don't think I'm complaining. But they are also modern First World problems. Overwhelm of technology and social media can steal your time and suck you into the void of indecision-nothingness. We need to simplify mundane areas of our lives, so we can make complex decisions more freely in important areas of our lives. Step 1 is to realize the anatomy of a decision, and its ease and simplicity. The anatomy of a decision:

1 Option A
2 Option B
3 Option A + B
4 Neither Option A nor B

Reduce all complexity. Focus on these four possible decision scenarios. Invest a little time upfront to either outsource or systemize all non-vital decisions, taking a little time once to remove decision fatigue forever. I asked my 'Disruptive Entrepreneur' Facebook community what areas of life they had little 'hacks' to reduce decision fatigue in, so you can set these up to reduce overwhelm and time wastage in as many areas as possible:

1 Save routes to regular destinations on sat nav
2 Wear similar clothes (put them out the night before. Or have your wife choose for you, as my business partner Mark Homer is so very proud of.)
3 Shop where possible in bulk for months or more of stock
4 Save regular items on online shopping
5 Put keys, headphones and other items you lose in the same place every time
6 Having a secure passwords app for all private data you need to access
7 Decide your meal plan a week in advance (and to save your Deliveroo bills!)
8 Batch tasks together to avoid time wasted by task jumping (such as emails, calls, tidying, errands, meetings and so on)
9 Get rid of all clutter from sight and organize all stock and files for easy access
10 Run your day with a diary rather than your day running you
11 Stick with the same brands (phone, PC/Mac, etc.) so you don't have to relearn how to use new systems and software
12 Make important decisions and actions early in the day or in your 'zone' time
13 Commit yourself to a few, important 'causes'
14 Pick your battles selectively and wisely
15 Buy all gifts for the year in one shopping trip
16 Let other people worry for you

17 Use templates and checklists for more complex tasks for consistency and efficiency
18 Schedule 'routined' times for tasks such as exercise, meal times (especially raising kids)
19 Get coaches, trainers and/or mentors to stop you quitting or making excuses
20 Use review sites for travel and purchases
21 Synchronize access across all devices and tech of emails, folders, communication apps, invoices, receipts and documents
22 Save important dates and appointments in advance and 'recur' them in your diary

Start Now sound bite

The paradox of choice is that too many choices can create overwhelm and decision fatigue. Simplify all mundane areas of your life so that you have time and energy for important decisions. Look to set up systems or outsource all low-value, time-intensive tasks from the list above. For more like this, see the thread in the 'Disruptive Entrepreneurs' community group on Facebook: www.facebook.com/groups/DisruptiveEntrepreneursCommunity

22

Diminish the importance, remove the permanence

The bigger you make a decision and the more pressure you put on yourself to get it right or, worse, perfect, the harder it becomes to get it right. And you never get it perfect anyway. Look at the England football team.

In the research study *Why do English players fail in soccer penalty shootouts? A study of team status, self-regulation, and choking under pressure*, Geir Jordet wrote, 'the biggest problem for the English team is pressure from the surroundings. English players are exposed to far more pressure compared to players from other countries. The English culture is characterized by its focus on high expectations. English media has placed unrealistic expectations on the shoulders of the national football team in front of every tournament they have been involved in. Also, English players do not necessarily have the greatest skills, which make the high expectations even more unrealistic' (Journal of Sports Sciences, 2009).

And according to *Twelve Yards: The Art and Psychology of the Perfect Penalty*, by Ben Lyttleton, 'England is more likely to lose a shoot-out in its next tournament because it had lost its last two shoot-outs'.

Imagine the pressure as an England footballer. The entire nation and decades of history all placed squarely on your shoulders. The paradox is that this just makes it worse. In order to get yourself in a good place to 'Start Now. Get Perfect Later', you need to do the complete opposite. As Bob Rotella, sport and golf psychologist and author of *Golf is not a game of perfect* says: 'Practice like it's a competition so you can compete like it's a practice session'.

According to Martin Turner, a lecturer in Sport and Exercise Psychology at Staffordshire University, your ability to handle pressure situations (real, or imagined), is how you react to it. When you enter into a high-pressure situation, it's important that you're able to focus on the task. If you're so busy worrying about how you're going to perform, you'll waste essential brain power. Ironically, one of the ways most of us try to approach a stressful situation is by telling ourselves, 'Don't mess up' or 'Don't fail'. However, saying 'Don't fail' actually increases the chances that you'll fail. A vast amount of research shows that telling yourself not to do something actually – and ironically – increases the likelihood of you doing it.

The initial response to stress occurs unconsciously and automatically based on our initial rapid evaluation of the situation. Some people are able to respond in a manner that helps their performance, known as a 'challenge' state. Others enter into the 'threat' state, which has similar effects as the 'challenge' state such as heart rate increases. But this time, the blood vessels constrict, which means the blood pumped from the heart remains largely unchanged. As a result, the delivery of glucose and oxygen to the brain; which is essential to peak performance, is inefficient and our ability to focus and make decisions is hindered.

Turning a 'threat' (state) into a 'challenge' (state) is both a great way to handle a big task or tough situation, and a way to control your unconscious, natural, neurological responses.

Here are some ways to handle important tasks and decisions:

1. Remove the permanence

In 100 years, or maybe a week, the hard decision you face now will mean nothing. It won't matter. You can change any decision the moment you've made it anyway, so no decisions are permanent,* even though they may feel it at the time. You can pivot anytime and no decision is or has to be final.

2. Diminish the importance

It's only a penalty. It's not life or death. See the current task for what it is, and not for what it's been built up to be. Get in the moment. Isolate the action or decision to the very small single thing that it is and you not only focus on it better but block out all distractions around it too.

3. Contextualize the decision

Presidents have to deal with people dying based on the decisions they have to make daily. Sometimes they have to decide between some people dying, or other people dying. Yours are nowhere near as likely to carry such consequences. It will help you to remember this.

4. Balance your expectations

The more unrealistic your expectations are, the harder they are to live up to. The greater the gap between where you are and

---

*...no decisions are permanent. The more anal-ytical of you may state: 'Rob, murder is permanent. Chopping off your leg is permanent.' Yes, you got me on that one! Please don't go and take these actions and then come back to me and ask me how to make these decisions non-permanent. These are actions from your decisions, and these can't be retracted. I suggest virtually all decisions are non-permanent, but for the few that are, be mindful of the permanence of them.

where you want to be, the more frustrated you can be. Set the big goal, then let it go and focus on small, single tasks. Then reward and congratulate yourself frequently by achieving the small wins, as they lead to the big ones.

5. Take your art seriously, but not yourself

Be serious about your work, but not yourself and how you approach life. Have fun. Be playful. Chill out a bit. Enjoy the moment and do not delay your happiness into the future that never comes.

6. Figure it out as you go, not before you go

You are infinitely resourceful, creative and dynamic. Allow this to come through by starting now and getting perfect later. No one has all the answers at first. It's never too late to start but it's always too late to wait.

Start Now sound bite

The more important or, worse, permanent you trick yourself into believing a decision is, the more pressure you put yourself under unnecessarily. This can build up and, like England taking penalties, will manifest in pressure, stress and failure. In time, all decisions will matter less, or not at all, so reduce the importance and permanence using the six easy strategies above.

23
Don't fake it till you make it, do this instead...

There's a popular saying that I don't like. It's 'Fake it till you make it'.

I don't think you should 'fake' anything. I know where this is coming from; you have to think it before you can become it. You have to visualize yourself having, winning or completing the thing before you've done the thing. But faking? Really?

I don't think you need to do that. Any person with integrity is going to struggle to fake it, because you will feel a fraud and it is not who you really are. But...

...if you do not think about what you want to bring about before it comes about you will go without.

See what I did there? I think the ideal balance of staying true to who you are, but wanting to become a better person, with better skills, and better results, is best achieved by a replacement of the quote 'fake it till you make it' (which probably only came about because it conveniently rhymes) with 'be it till you see it'.

Virtually all good athletes, actors and highly successful people do this all the time. They either strategically visualize (like seeing the shot go in, or the fight or competition won before the result has happened), or they have been dreaming about it unconsciously for years. This builds a great magnetic attraction towards the desired outcome. The mind has the infinite power to bring about what you think about. So be careful and strategic with what you think about.

Einstein said, 'Imagination is more important than knowledge'. Get into the mindset of 'be it till you see it', by taking control of your thought processes to visualize, think about and wish for what you want, not what you don't. Your mind only sees what you see. If you see or ask for what you *don't* want, it sees what you don't want, and focuses on what you don't want.

I wonder if you have ever wished for a partner who was *not* like your last one. Only to get one who was so different from your last one that you didn't want them?! I wonder if you have wished to be less busy, only to feel bored and not valued? I wonder if you have wished to have more on, only to be completely overwhelmed? These last two are my recurring loops. Busy to bored to busy to bored to busy to bored, because when I'm too busy I wish it all away, and when I'm too bored I wish it all back. I always get exactly what I ask for. You'd think I'd learn, right?

Start Now sound bite

Get very clear about what you want. Visualize consciously and unconsciously. Then act 'as if' you are already there: being, doing and having it. Not as a fake, but as an authentic person moving towards where you want to go and who you want to become. 'Be it till you see it'. Practise, don't pretend.

24
Think BIG, start small

To help you diminish the importance and remove the permanence of any (big) decision, start with the simple first step. How
do you eat an elephant? One bite at a time. By all means set
your big target to motivate yourself towards greatness, but don't
allow that to overwhelm you. Put your big goal out there, then
let it go. Start with the very first, small step. Acorns grow into
oak trees. The journey of a thousand miles starts with a single
step. You probably know all the clichés, but *to know and not to
do is not to know*.

Make big decisions with your heart but small decisions with
your head. It might be hard to write a book, but it's easy to
write the first paragraph. It might be hard to lose 10 pounds,
but it's easy to replace the fries with a salad.

If you take care of the present moment, being in the moment,
then the future takes care of itself. You gain momentum
moment by moment. Many people start their diet tomorrow,
but tomorrow never comes. And sometimes they empty the
entire fridge into their gob on Sunday night, so they can start
tomorrow. And then they never do. Mañana. So 'Start Now. Get
Perfect Later'.

If you watch the Truck Pull event in the World's Strongest
Man competition, even the biggest guys in the world take a
long time and a huge amount of vein-popping effort just to
get the truck moving inch by inch. But they keep on pulling. They look like they're struggling to get nowhere. But they

keep pulling. Small step by small step. Small pull by small pull. Once they get a bit of momentum, the truck gains speed and then the momentum of the truck takes over and, like an oil tanker turning, is virtually impossible to stop. And so it is for your 'Think BIG, start small' task. *By the yard it's hard, by the inch it's a cinch.*

Start Now sound bite

Think BIG, sure, but start small, so you can start now. The bigger the task, the harder it is to start. Chunk it down to the single, easy first step, and start walking. Before you know it, you've run a marathon or eaten an elephant.

25
Let go to grow

In order to grow, you must let go. Let go of control. Let go of perfectionism. Let go of responsibility. Let go of your baggage. *You have a finite, limited amount of time and energy in your very short lifetime.* How you invest it will determine the happiness and success you experience in that scarily short amount of time.

Here are some ways to get more done in less time. Let go to grow, to worry and control less and be more happy:

1. Don't sweat the small stuff

Most things are not worth worrying about or giving as much attention as you might be giving. Anything that doesn't take you closer towards your vision and goals, or isn't high on your values, just let it be. You can't grow the big stuff if you sweat the small stuff.

2. Know what you can control and what you can't

You can't control everything, and you certainly can't control everyone (or anyone). You are in control of your decisions and actions, and inspiring others into action, but from there you have to let go of control, or you'll push everyone away from you. There's a paradox in control versus faith. Sure, you can control the goal or target, to some degree, say for your staff, but you can't control exactly how they get there. Set the outcome, but let go of the process to get there and let people (staff, kids, colleagues) get on with it and find their own way. They will be more empowered and take responsibility themselves this way.

3. Pick your battles wisely

Fight your own battles. Leave everything else. There are too many battles for you to be able to commit to. They can drain you. If people see you picking battles with everyone, they will soon tune out to your message. There are a handful of things that you really believe in, stand for, and want to inspire others to believe. Invest most of your time into those, and let the rest go. Move on. Nothing to see here. These are not the droids you are looking for.

4. What gives you a return and what drains you

There are many things that can have the illusion of being worthy of your time but, in fact, drain, waste or distract you. Your time-energy is either being compounded or eroded. Know what decision or action is worth your time, and what is not. Check that each decision or task gives you value, progress, results, happiness and fulfilment.

5. KRAs and IGTs (Key Result Areas and Income Generating Tasks)

If you've read my previous books *Money* and *Life Leverage*, you will know what KRAs and IGTs are. You can find definitions in Chapter 31. Time should be invested where possible, and not spent or wasted.

6. Trust the people you've decided to trust

If you've given people your faith and confidence, then show them by treating them with respect and autonomy. Sure, be there to support and guide, but show that you trust them by letting them crack on in their own style and allow them to do meaningful work that inspires them. Which leads to the next point...

7. Don't micro-manage

No one wants to be told what to do and then constantly interrupted and criticized. Sure, when training people, teach them. But let them try to do it to themselves. The best way to teach is not just to show but to let them have a go. If you set them off on a task, constantly getting in their way will only demotivate them. Might they make mistakes, on your watch? Yes. Have you in the past? Yes. You can't grow without the help and leverage of others. You want them motivated and inspired, and they will get this through their own achievement. You had faith and trust to get them started, so let them finish.

8. Give control to gain control

The best way to have control, is to give responsibility to smart people and treat them well. The more you need something, the more it controls you. Manage the control versus faith paradox. Let other people take the credit. Let other people grow under your gentle guidance and they will flourish, and you will win.

Start Now sound bite

You have to let go to grow. The more you try to control the situation, and people, the more you push them away. Tension causes friction, and friction slows things down. Manage the paradox of control versus faith, set the goal, then trust people you've decided to trust, and let them crack on. Be there for support but don't get in their way. Pick your battles wisely.

26
Your decision muscle

Your ability to make fast, yet considered, smart decisions is like a muscle that can be trained. It can grow. It's a practice, not an identity. No one is either all good or all bad at making decisions. We are all good at making good decisions in areas we have practised and gained experience. You carry the experience of past good and bad decisions to draw from. You build up your intuition and sixth sense for the situation through all the previous times you've been there.

You've shown it already in areas of confidence and experience that you can make great decisions. Everything great about your life has come about through the great decisions you made. So now that you know you can, you can carry that confidence into other areas and transmute the intuition you have into areas where you are procrastinating or overwhelmed. Here are seven actions you can implement to build your decision muscle like Arnold Schwarzenegger's biceps:

1. Take baby steps in your decision-making process

Ancient martial artists used to improve the strength in their legs and ability to leap by jumping in and out of holes dug in the ground. They would very slowly and progressively make the hole a small amount deeper, so slowly that their muscles didn't even notice the change. Then they'd wear one extra t-shirt, again so light that their muscles didn't even notice. They would progressively gain strength and power without fatigue. And so it can be with your decision making muscle. Take small steps towards bigger decisions, and soon you'll be making big, fast decisions without even noticing it.

2. Get mentors and support to stress test your decisions first

Sometimes you can't solve problems yourself, because it was your thought process and decision making that created the problem in the first place. It is a strength and not a weakness to seek out support, guidance and mentorship. Find those more experienced than you in the area of challenge or big decision. Find people who have been doing it so long they could make the decision in a nanosecond. Request their counsel. Then let go and have faith that the decision is right. This is often the quickest and easiest way to make a great decision.

3. Give yourself a deadline to do all the research you need

You will never be armed with all the knowledge you require to be perfect before you start. But you could get 70% to 80% of the research and diligence done up front. Set yourself a deadline where you will 100% commit to the decision and do all the necessary background work to be as informed as you can. Then on the deadline, make the decision. This, in turn, will train your decision muscle to be faster and stronger next time, as you bank the experience.

4. Review decisions after the fact to learn from them

Take time afterwards to reverse analyse your decisions, to review what worked and what could have been done better. Fill that bank of experience. Too many people just keep making the same mistakes, missing the lessons hidden in plain sight. When you review a decision after the moment, you are in a different emotional place and, as such, can review it in a different, possibly clearer and more balanced way.

5. Learn from everyone: listen more and talk less...

...as Napoleon Hill explains: 'Keep your eyes and ears wide open – and your mouth closed – if you wish to acquire the habit of prompt decisions. Those who talk too much do little else. If you talk more than you listen, you not only deprive yourself of many opportunities to accumulate useful knowledge, but you also disclose your plans and purposes to people who will take great delight in defeating you, because they envy you. Your actions count more than your words. Tell the world what you intend to do, but first show it' (*Think and Grow Rich*).

6. Embrace the perceived mistakes as part of the process...

...as they may be your biggest successes. Coca-Cola was intended as medicine. The Post-It Note was a failed glue and the fungus that makes penicillin was grown accidentally in an uncleaned petri dish. Almost all heavy metal is played on de-tuned guitars! See every decision as a test and you will discover new and surprising results.

7. Keep deciding (it's never over)

Just because you made a good (or bad) decision, doesn't mean it's over and done with. Every decision almost immediately needs to be followed up with another decision. And so it continues.

This keeps you balanced between humble and cocky. Never think you've made it just because you made a good decision, and never think it's over just because you made a bad one.

As you get better at making good decisions, righting your wrong decisions and learning from all decisions, you will become a great problem solver. This will inspire others to be great decision makers and action takers too, and the greatest single strength of a leader is inspiring and creating other leaders. Problem solvers rule the world, as you will discover towards the end.

Start Now sound bite

Decision making is a muscle that can be trained and can grow strong. Learn from all decisions, good and bad, and you will get better and faster at making them. Transmute your confidence from other areas of your life, seek counsel of those who've got experience, and keep tweaking your decisions embracing perceived mistakes; they could be the next Post-It Note or penicillin.

SECTION 4
To do, or not to do?

27
What is decisiveness?

To decide, or not to decide, that is the question. Maybe you should take more time to think about that before you make a decision? Er, no.

Decisiveness is the (leadership) trait that gives you:

1 'the ability to make decisions quickly and effectively' (Dictionary.com)
2 'the conclusive nature of an issue that has been settled or a result that has been produced' (Dictionary.com)
3 (the ability to) 'draw heavily on past experiences to influence how it (the current decision) is implemented' (earlbreon.com)
4 'the spark that ignites action. The courageous facing of issues, knowing that if they are not faced, problems will remain forever unanswered' (Wilferd A. Peterson)

Decisiveness seems to be both inherent in all success, and a pre-requisite for it. But we often make it so much harder and more complicated than it really is. Anyone can be decisive, because all you need to do is say 'yes' or 'no' to something. And sometimes saying 'wait' to something is acceptable, because deciding to wait or deciding to do nothing is still a decision. Your ever-improving skills in making good decisions are based on how effectively you choose from the only four options of the anatomy of any decision:

1 Option A
2 Option B
3 Option A + B
4 Neither Option A nor B

Keep it simple.

Start Now sound bite

Decisiveness is the (leadership) trait that gives you the ability to make the right actions towards a desired outcome quickly and effectively. It draws on past experience that can be built up and it is the courageous facing of issues, igniting action towards success.

28
What NOT to do

If you are a little stuck with what you *should* be doing, working out and picking off what you *should not* be doing is a valuable pre-action action. There are two forms of what NOT to do:

1   Time wasting/unimportant tasks
2   Tasks that you leverage out to others

1. Time wasting/unimportant tasks

Should be obvious, but worth listing out. Too much time on social media, long meetings, forum debates, getting sucked in by haters and trolls, pity-parties, selfies and foodies, small talk, arguments, having to be right, allowing interruptions, surfing online, checking email, low-value admin, tidying up and cleaning, checking the fridge (one of my undiagnosed OCD traits), TV or YouTube, micro-managing, and general avoidance and active procrastination tasks should be avoided. You know what you *should not* be doing, so stop doing it.

Brian Tracy, motivational public speaker and self-development expert/author, calls these 'posteriorities'. The opposite of priorities. The lowest-value, most time-draining and revenue-sucking tasks known to man. Most people say procrastination is a bad thing, but procrastination is a *great* thing on low IGT tasks. Be lazy, unmotivated, bored and apathetic to all of these; avoid or outsource. Doing these posteriorities and convincing yourself that you are busy and working hard is no different to procrastination, other than it is active and takes ages. Beware of this self-delusion that your split personality will try to convince you of. It is a liar. You are getting nowhere, but boy does it take a long time to get there.

Parkinson's Law states 'work expands to fill the time available for its completion'. If you don't prioritize and posteriorize, then all tasks become equal and fill the same amount of time and space. However, no two tasks are equal. Some take longer than others and some are more important than others. If you allow unimportant tasks to take priority over IGTs, they will fill all the time you have, and there will be no space left to do the most important and highest-leverage tasks.

2. Tasks that you leverage out to others

If you want to grow, you have to let go. If you want to scale, DIY will make you fail. Be it low-value admin or high-value IGTs, you need the help of others to get your task list down yet get your done list up. Just as every master was once a disaster, so every big business owner, manager or successfully scaled person has the help of assistants, staff, carers, outsourcers, coaches and mentors. You can achieve this one of two ways:

i. You start or make part of the decision

You make the initial decision or take the first action step, like setting a budget for a department to spend, then allow them to spend it as they see fit. You trust them to make the smartest decisions, within the initial parameters you set up at the start.

ii. You let them make all the decisions

You bypass step i. They make all the decisions, you just give them the task. They set the budget and spend the budget.

In order to successfully leverage out tasks in your 'to do' list, you need to rethink and rename what a 'to do' list even is. And so we move to the next chapter...

Start Now sound bite

It can help knowing what you should be doing by knowing what you should NOT be doing. Minimize all low-value and time-wasting tasks, and conversely leverage out high-value tasks that others can do better than you, to get your task list down and your done list up.

29
Busy, productive or efficient?

Busy is working hard and doing lots. Productive is getting the important things done. Efficient is getting the important things done in the shortest amount of time. Knowing the difference, and knowing yourself, will reduce your busyness and increase your efficiency. Sometimes, doing less of the wrong things and a little bit of the right, most important things can greatly increase your efficiency.

To know how to become efficient requires you to know where you are busy but unproductive or, worse, wasteful. Perry Marshall (American entrepreneur and author) taught me to write a simple work log, noting down exactly how I spent my time, in blocks (usually 30 minutes). It was a game changer for me when I did this in 2007, and I'd strongly encourage you to do the same thing.

For the next two weeks, keep a work and energy log. A simple notes document or even old-skool journal will do, jotting down each task. Note down what you did, when (how long) you did it, what it was (work, play, rest, specific task), and how you felt about it. (Were you in the zone? Was it a struggle? Did you enjoy it?) Keep this really simple by having a key or code system. You could set up a template in Microsoft Word or on a spreadsheet, so you fill it in the same way each day. Write a really brief description as above, perhaps with 1-10 scores or letters for how you felt and how much you enjoyed it, and if it was (W)ork, (R)est, (P)lay and so on. Here's an example to get you started:

TIME	TASK*	DETAILS	ENERGY*	AREA*

* Task: **W** for Work / **S** for Social / **R** for Rested
* Energy: **L** for Lethargic / **S** for Steady / **E** for Energised / **F** for on Fire
* Area: **KLA** for Key Life Areas / **KRA** for Key Results Area / **IGT** for Income Generating Task / **A** for Admin / **W** for Wasted

Two weeks seems to be long enough to get good consistent data, but not too long to be a chore. You will know the right amount of time. You will get amazing insight into your daily cycles and routines. Your highs and lows, ebbs and flows. Your time invested, spent and wasted; and where your 80/20 maximum results come from and the things that distract you the most. You will discover when you are on fire and when the carb-coma kicks in and how long it lasts. You will discover when you like to be alone, when you like to socialize, when you prefer to work and when you feel playful, and when you are inspired. It will all be there in front of your eyes. You might even become more efficient just doing this exercise, because you won't want to read it back full of wasted effort and distractions.

You can then re-organize your time, diary and placement of tasks for maximum and ruthless efficiency. You can batch similar types of tasks together to minimize the warm-up phase and maximize the in-flow stage. You can run meetings back-to-back-to-back in one day. You can make sure you have everything you need on your laptop so you can get all tasks done from anywhere in the world without having to be tied to the office. You can have all logins to hand to avoid searching for them. You can do all your calls while on the road in one time chunk, and so on. More on this coming soon.

Start Now sound bite

Keep a two-week work log to discover when you are busy, productive and efficient. Know the difference between the three for 5× or 10× the results in one fifth or one tenth of the time.

30
'To leverage' lists

We need to rethink, and rename, the age-old 'to do' list. Giving it that name sets you up for failure, because it is giving bad advice. Many things on your 'to do' list, you shouldn't actually 'do' at all.

Have you ever written a 'to do' list, and then looked at the list and wanted to puke up all over it? Just the list makes you feel sick, let alone the tasks on it. It looks like some sort of ancient scroll. And then you pick off a few 'quick wins' on the list, just to make yourself feel better that you can cross a couple of things off (even though those quick wins had zero importance). And then you remember something you did earlier and you write it on the list just so that you can cross it back off! Ah, that feels good, another one done! Ha!

'To do' lists can turn you insane. Handle with extreme care. Some people are such perfectionists and list-tickers that if they don't cross everything off their list, they will overheat and have a full-on meltdown. Over a *list*. All their happiness in their entire life reliant on that one single list. Here are some tips to manage your lists more effectively, before we move onto a full redesign:

1. Order them from importance/priority down

Self-explanatory, but be honest with yourself. If you don't prioritize importance, you'll end up having to prioritize emergencies.

2. Do your list the night before

It wraps the end of the day nicely in a bow. It empties your mind so you can switch off, be satisfied and sleep well. It means you can have the fastest start to the next day possible. Doing your list the night before also means you can take time to prioritize tasks, before the demands of the day suck you in.

3. Never start the next item until you've finished the current item

It's tempting to task jump, pick off a couple of perceived quick wins, give yourself some variety and avoid the hard task. Do not be tempted; you'll end up scatter-gunning yourself all over the place.

4. If you want to add something, what will you take away?

Negotiate with yourself. Have a maximum number of allowable tasks on your list and set a rule of one-in-one-out.

5. Keep the list to a few items only (Post-It Note)

The temptation to keep adding to the list will be great as you get busier. Set a maximum of five to seven tasks on your list. If you have more that come in, note them somewhere else and put them on reserve. When you start this, there will be the odd emergency that comes in but, over time, you will get the important tasks done before they become emergencies and starve the fires of oxygen before they start.

There's a nice easy system I wrote about in *Life Leverage* called the '4D System':

1 Delegate
2 Delete
3 Delay
4 Do

You should follow one of these 4Ds when you get a task fall into your lap. You should go through the 4Ds in this order, with the idea that by the time you get to 'Do', the last 'D', you will have cleared many of those tasks already, reduced your overwhelm, and only have the important and high IGT tasks left on your desk.

Sometimes if I have some big 'frogs' (big hairy tasks), or tasks I perceive to be long or hard, I can procrastinate on starting them. As the deadline draws near, it starts to occupy a larger space in my mind and produces anxiety. As that pressure builds, I look for more creative solutions, and often end up asking for help, delegating or leveraging out the task completely. This gives me a great sense of relief, but then I ask myself the question: 'Why didn't I do that at the start?' Hence the order of the 4Ds, to help you be more productive and efficient. Most people do them the wrong way around always starting with 'Do'.

I used to edit my books myself, do all the research, design the covers, write the bio and back cover text, struggle with titles and sub-titles on my own. I even used to try to typeset the entire book. What an idiot I was:

1 I am useless at these tasks
2 They produce anxiety and stress in me
3 That makes me procrastinate and feel overwhelmed

4 It stops me doing: (a) what I am good at (writing stream of consciousness) and (b) what I should be doing (writing stream of consciousness)
5 There are people I have access to who are WAY better than me at these tasks

Duh.

Don't be like (the old) me. Be more self-aware. Follow these systems and use this reworked 'to do' list that I call a 'to leverage' list, following the L1 M2 DL formula:

1 Leverage 1st
2 Manage 2nd
3 Do LAST!

Leverage	Manage	Do

When you're busy, perhaps the first thing you think is 'What do I need to do?' or 'I've got so much to do, where do I even start?' Or 'When can I get this done?' or 'How can I even do this?'

Now try this: next time you start your task or 'to do' list, instead of starting with a task, start with what you can leverage or outsource. Who can you get to do the first task you were going to do? And the second. And the third. Like researching and editing and typesetting this book.

Out of seven tasks for the day, if you've leveraged four of them, and you do three of them, you'll achieve more than double the results in less than half of the time. *And* you will improve the quality of the output. Genius.

Once you've leveraged out tasks you would ordinarily have done yourself, they don't just magically arrive on your desk the next day in shiny wrapping paper and a bow. Any task 'leveraged' needs managing through to completion. Check through your leveraged tasks and guide or manage them through to completion. Only once you have gone through these two steps should you even consider 'doing' a task. A few small hours moved from 'doing' to 'leveraging' has huge compounded benefits. You might end up leveraging three tasks, having two 'under manage-ment' and only two that you actually have to do yourself.

And if you're too busy to invest time, that's probably the very reason you need to do it. And if no one can do that task or job as well as you, that's probably the very reason you need to do it too.

Start Now sound bite

Use the 4Ds system of Delegate, Delete, Delay before you Do. Reduce your 'to do' list by up to two-thirds by leveraging first, managing second and doing last or not at all. Outsource all the things you aren't good at, that distract you and you don't enjoy to others who love it and are better at it. Rename your 'to do' list your 'to leverage' list to change your habits.

31

It's not what you do, it's when you do it

All this 5am club posting on social media is, frankly, nonsense. In the world of personal development in some fraternities you are seen as a total loser and non-hustler unless you get up at 5am. There's also a 6am club. And a 4am club. I used to get IN at these times, let alone get UP!

I'd read in a lot of business books that successful people, such as Michelle Obama or Dwayne 'The Rock' Johnson (both of whom I admire), would get up at 4am and only have five hours' sleep a night. I used to think that I needed to do the same to be successful. And then I'd feel guilty or like a loser any time I got up after that time or slept for eight hours.

I got so sick of all the pulling in different directions by myself and the influencers I was following, that I decided to test it for myself. I also encouraged others in communities I was in, to see if there was an optimum time to go to bed, get up, how much sleep to have, and when we are most productive.

Here are the findings: we are all different. The results weren't scientific, but they don't need to be. I tested going to bed late and getting up late. Going to bed early and getting up early. Even going to bed late and getting up early. I tested what the best coffee was for me, how it made me feel and what times I drunk it. I tested specific amounts of sleep and chunks of time in the day I felt the most energized and the most lethargic. I'll share my findings, but the point of this is to test yourself and find your own ideal flow, sleep/wake and energy cycle, or circadian rhythm.

Very active people, through their nature or job or work-outs, need more sleep than those who are more still in body and mind. My optimum is 9:30pm to 5:30am or 9:45pm to 5:45am. I could handle seven hours' sleep as long as it is occasionally, but six hours or less and I'll feel like I have a 15-pint hangover the next day. Any later than 11pm to bed and I'll feel like I had a 15-vodka hangover and a UFC fight. I do know of people who get less sleep, but I don't know if it works for them, or they are building sleep debt to then burn out. I never lie in because I never need to catch up with sleep, unless jet-lagged of course.

My optimum times for coffee are 6am and 11:30am. The same type (medium Costa Coffee – should be getting a sponsorship deal from them! – skinny cappuccino extra shot). I tested all coffee types and this one gives me the least amount of 'crash' and feels the most like a class A, clean drug hit (not that I know, but from what I see in the movies!). I've done the same testing with food but won't bore you with the details. Alcohol doesn't work for me, so I quit. But it does relax some people, in small quantities, so all good if that works for you. If you know two will work but three will give you a hangover the next day: Only. Drink. Two.

Overlaid with these times are highest and lowest energy ebbs and flows. For me, 6am to 8am are very high energy time slots, and so I schedule high KRA and IGT work then. I have likely written 80% of this book in this time slot, and the 20% in the rest of the day has probably taken me the same amount of time. Another energy high comes between 11am and 1pm, and so high KRA and IGT work go in there. Family time, dinner every night at home, golf with my son Bobby and my daughter Ariana all go in the next highest energy slots and/or time zones that dictate (such as before school or dinner after school). Calls and meetings fit around this, and then no work, meetings or decision responsibility go in the low times between 10:30 and 11:30am, and after 3pm. Workouts move in gaps based on where I need a pick up, but never after 5:30pm as I always talk myself out of working out after dinner.

If I *only* worked in the 6am to 8am slot, virtually all the work I need to do for the day is done. I often send out all my leverage tasks at this point too. Mundane admin or emails, or replies to people that are not urgent or high IGT, I will do in the downtime after dinner. When I travel I have a driver so I can leverage the time. I get my 6am coffee myself and put podcasts on in the car on 2× speed.

KRAs (Key Result Areas) are the highest-value areas that you focus on to achieve your vision. They are the three to seven areas in which you should invest most of your time to make the maximum difference to your team, your role and your legacy. IGTs (Income-Generating Tasks) are tasks of the highest value to you (or your company) that align with and serve your KRAs. They are the tasks that bring the highest, leveraged results directly related to income, in the optimum amount of time, bringing maximum benefit and minimum wastage. IGTs get more done and more earned in less time.

You shouldn't care about my daily rhythm, but you should care enough about yours to test it yourself. I can say that so many people I coach and mentor, who struggle with time management, overwhelm and prioritization, have not properly created their ideal daily diary structure like this. Remember that 'to know and not to do is not to know'. I'd say this testing took me three months all in, and has made a huge impact in my life. If you do the same, it will help you:

1 Get way more done in less time
2 Get your best KRA and IGT work done
3 Get your best KRA and IGT work done EARLY...
4 ...therefore, you get momentum and feel good and get even more done
5 Prioritize important family and social or hobby time
6 Get the ideal work/life balance for you
7 Stay healthy, focused and mostly happy
8 Live on your terms and not run ragged by everyone else

My wife and I diarize date nights and nights to watch Netflix documentaries. I schedule golf with my son. I eat at the same time every day. I need to schedule in more sex between 8:30pm and 8:31pm, but otherwise the system works beautifully! I am not a structured person generally, I like freedom and variety, but ironically this discipline and routine gives me more freedom.

If there's ONE ACTION you take from this book, it is to test and create your daily routine based on: time you go to bed, time you get up, what you eat and drink, when you eat and drink it, and where you fit in your work, rest and play accordingly. It will make you ruthlessly effective and efficient, and it wouldn't be an exaggeration to say you could get 5× the work done in one fifth of the time to become 10× as effective.

Start Now sound bite

It's not what you do, it's when you do it. Test your ideal daily structure by testing your optimum sleep, diet and where you place your tasks in the day according to your highs and lows, ebbs and flows. Test a few routines; see how productive, efficient and balanced they make your day, and settle on the ideal one for you. Plan your entire schedule: work, rest and play based on this and live life on your own terms.

32
The Pomodoro Technique

This is a time management philosophy that aims to provide you with maximum focus and creative freshness, allowing you to complete projects faster with less mental fatigue or distractions. It is based on the studies by Francesco Cirillo (an expert on time management), who found he wasn't retaining or working effectively, despite studying all night. After realizing he was getting distracted and not using his study time efficiently, he grabbed a tomato-shaped kitchen timer (*pomodoro* is Italian for 'tomato'), set it for 10 minutes, and tried working solidly for those 10 minutes without doing *anything* else. It forced him to focus before rewarding him with a break and helped him get more done, even with the break time added in.

There are two elements to the Pomodoro Technique:

1 You work in short sprints, which ensures you're consistently productive
2 You take regular breaks that bolster your motivation and keep you creative

When faced with any large task or series of tasks, break the work down into short, timed intervals (called 'Pomodoros') that are spaced out by short breaks. This trains your brain to focus for short periods, but with ruthless and intense productivity.

I use this technique in many areas, especially when writing. 25 minutes on, five-minute break, in sets of three, with a longer break after the set of three. When I take people away to my once a year 'Book Writing Bootcamp', we do four sets of three each day, so 12 sets of 25 minutes. Most people get 6,000 to 15,000 words a day done. It works. There are five simple steps:

1 Choose a task to be accomplished
2 Set the Pomodoro (timer) to 25 minutes
3 Work on the task until the timer rings
4 Take a short break (five minutes or so; don't be tempted to work through)
5 Every three to four Pomodoros, take a longer break – say 15-20 minutes

If you're distracted part-way through, you either end the Pomodoro there, save your work and start a new one later, or you have to postpone the distraction until the Pomodoro is complete. If you isolate yourself from distractions, then you don't get distracted!

Start Now sound bite

The Pomodoro Technique is a simple 25 minutes on, five minutes break system to get deep, focused work done. Isolate yourself from distraction, focus on your 25 minutes and you will become ruthlessly productive, even factoring in the break times. This has helped me write more than a book a year for nearly a decade and can help you; Get. Shit. Done.

SECTION 5

Who's the easiest person to lie to…?

…(yourself)

33
Latent resourcefulness

You are the easiest person to lie to.

Whether you beat yourself up that you're not good enough (a lie), or you delude yourself that it doesn't matter when it does (a lie), or you let yourself off the hook. One of the biggest lies you tell yourself is that you need to have everything ready before you start, and related to that is that you don't know if you can do it ('it' being new thing, scary thing or big hairy thing).

These are lies. And here's why:

You and every other human being on this planet are infinitely resourceful and creative. Everything that we know and take for granted in the material world was created by fellow man, from a single thought or idea. A tiny seed of inspiration that came from the ether, where someone used their resourcefulness, desire, creativity and work ethic to turn it into the material.

If one person can do that, any and every person can do that, in their areas of highest value and interest. No, you can't grow three extra feet by thinking it in your mind, but if it is humanly possible, you can do it too.

The paradoxical void many people get stuck in is the void between the comfortable known and the uncomfortable unknown. The comfortable known is safe, but all resourcefulness and creativity is latent and suppressed. The uncomfortable unknown is a bit scary, you don't feel ready, it's daunting, but that's where all your untapped infinite resources are stored ready and waiting. When needs must, you do. You always have. Don't leave all that creativity and problem solving in hibernation, get comfortably uncomfortable; 'Start Now. Get Perfect Later' and allow all that resourcefulness to flow out of you, to you and through you.

Being creative is much easier than most people think. Every human being is creative, not just the arty-creative types. There is creativity in the mundane as well as the artistic and visionary. Creativity is simply balancing the known with the unknown; the tangible with the ethereal, and the dance between the two. Here are some ways to be more creative, from a previous hippy-anti-capitalist-rage-against-the-system artist (that was me):

1 Listen to and watch very creative people (speakers, comedians, artists, entrepreneurs, etc.) and model their behaviours, and...

2 ...read their books. Listen to their audio books and podcasts. Go on their seminars and get mentored by them (where possible)

3 Isolate yourself from noise, media and negativity to allow ideas to come in

4 Ask for smart people's thoughts, ideas and advice

5 Talk less, listen more

6 Create hybrids: merge and piece together ideas from different niches (most new music genres are hybrids of existing ones)

7 Study innovations. Reverse engineer them. Follow proven processes

8 Exercise more. Fire off the endorphins and get the creative juices flowing

9 Travel to amazing places and experience different cultures

10 Seek out, accept and engage in continual feedback

11 Practise contrarianism, unconventional wisdom and left-field thinking. New spins on existing norms. Uncommon sense. How can you think differently or laterally?

12 How can you look at the same problem in a different way?

13 How would your idol or someone successful and creative solve the problem?

14 Isolate yourself in a creative space (detailed soon)

And finally...write, write, write. Get your thoughts, ideas and emotions out. Write when you've got ideas. Write when you're inspired. Write when you're stuck. Write when you're angry. Write when you're feeling guilty. Write when you're arguing with someone in your head. Or record yourself saying it out loud. It empties the brain to create new space for more inspiration. The ideas will just come out as you write.

Start Now sound bite

You are infinitely creative and resourceful. For most people, it is latent within them, bursting to come out if only given the chance. Get a little uncomfortable and follow one or more of the 15 points to being more creative, and all future solutions will come to you with least effort.

34
Gaming, tricking & second-guessing yourself

If you're the easiest person to lie to, you can also trick yourself when you lie to yourself. You can second-guess how you are going to feel and act in a future situation because it is a recurring trait or habit and, as such, trick yourself to avoid the temptation of distraction, procrastination and overwhelm.

The first step is to be self-aware and honest enough to know what you are doing. Some things, like walking the dog or having a coffee, can be both procrastination and motivation, depending how you use them. Don't lie to yourself, know the difference. Call yourself out. Don't make excuses for any nonsense. Admit it, you're procrastinating. Interrupt those excuses.

You are not too tired. You do not need to look in the fridge. You will not do it tomorrow. You do not need to check social media. You do not need to clean or tidy anything. You do not need another coffee. You do not need to walk the dog. You do not need to do your hair. You do not need to know, or plan, or research anymore. You do not need more money. You do not need to wait for the next recession or crash or financial meltdown to pass. And you definitely do not need all your fuckin' ducks in a row. Who has ducks on their wall anymore anyway?

All of these excuses are bollocks (and collated from one of my Facebook communities!), but the voices in your head and your alter-egos are going to nag away at you constantly with all these 'pain relief' excuses. But do you want a little pain now for a lot of pleasure later, or an easy 'let yourself off the hook' now for a long life of slow torture?

Here are some tips and tricks to 'game yourself' towards more proactive decisions:

1. Compartmentalize your diary (with advanced self-awareness)

As already covered, plan your diary knowing in advance your highs and lows, ebbs and flows of energy, productivity and time 'in the zone'. Template all your KRAs, IGTs, family, work, rest and play around this proven plan.

2. Know what gets you in the zone/state (and use it as a trigger)

Maybe coffee, or music (filthy heavy metal for me), a power work out, a walk in nature or a motivational YouTube video will get you all fired up and inspired? Use the one that works for you as a trigger by repeating it often. Once you have programmed your mind, the first split second of the trigger will automatically get you in that state.

3. Deadlines

Deadlines are hard enough for you to achieve with people you rely on, but on yourself they can be even harder. Game yourself by not only setting a deadline, but by setting the deadline before the actual deadline. Even if you miss it, you will have done much of the task, and you have time left you wouldn't have had.

Then you have to trick yourself into believing the first deadline and forget the fact that you have time left afterwards.

You can balance this trick with competitions, challenges, rewards and penalties. This works well managing and motivating others. To further trick yourself, cause some serious pain if you miss the deadline. As an example, I put a post on social media offering to pay all travel and accommodation expenses for some book critics to come and read and critique this book. I had over 120 requests. I reduced the number to 15 people. The date was set in stone, one week after the deadline I'd given myself to finish the first draft and a full read through. *If I don't get this done (shit, this date is nine days away!) then I either have to let down all those people, looking really stupid and messing them about; or pay a lot of money for people to read an unfinished book.* I used this strategy for *Money*, which is twice as long as this book, and it got the job done. It forced me to drag my arse through the pain and the voices and the excuses. This is possibly the single best trick to get important stuff done on time. You need some PAAAAIN!

4. Competitions and challenges

Have a little bet: for money or for sport. Challenge someone to a duel. For many people, the pain of getting their arse beaten is way stronger than money or other motivations. If you are a competitive psycho-nutter, this is a great way to game yourself. I have achieved six-packs in the past by having 30 or 60 day challenges with friends. When I say six pack, I mean I had great rib definition! I still won though! And even if I'd have lost, I'd have still won.

5. Rewards and penalties

What do you love to do, and what do you hate? Pick the most extreme cases of love and hate, and set a goal to either receive your reward, or accept your penalty. Rewards can be material but also experiential, and penalties can be public shaming, donations to causes you dislike or paying competitors money! PAIN!

6. Public declarations

The more people you tell about your goal and when you will achieve it, the more traction towards action you have. Many people don't do this through fear of failure, but doing this may reduce failure. If you don't want to look stupid in front of people, that's exactly the reason this trick works! Arnie was famous for telling everyone that he already was who he wanted to become, be it Mr Olympia or a Hollywood actor. He also shamed his calf muscles by wearing shorts all day every day, focusing his mind to build them up to a world champion size and definition. MORE PAIN!

7. Accountability

Take yourself and your lies out of the equation. Get a coach or mentor. Be in a community. Get an accountability partner or buddy. Be in mastermind groups. Set goals and have someone outside of yourself keep you accountable by nagging and bullying and stalking you into action. Easy to let yourself down, maybe not so easy to let others down. Want to make it even more painful? Pay them lots of money.

8. If in doubt, leverage it out

Get someone smarter and better and quicker to do the task for you. Save yourself all the pain, follow the L1 M2 DL model as set out in a previous chapter. Repeat after me: If. In. Doubt. Leverage. It. Out.

9. Continued self-testing

Test the above eight gaming techniques. Some will work for you, others not so much. Some will take some time, and you will discover your own with time. We all have different motivators to move towards and away from. Uncover yours and leverage them against yourself, you sado-masochist, you! Continue to gain traction towards action without distraction.

10. Isolate yourself

And this moves us nicely to the next chapter. Follow me…

But before you do, these 10 strategies work. They defeat your inner bas-tard and work when things get hard for you and other areas of list-making and prioritization have not worked for you. This chapter is the one you can come back to again and again as a reference if all the others are not working. *Game yourself to win the game.*

> **Start Now sound bite**
>
> *You are the easiest person to lie to, so second-guess how and when you will let yourself off the hook. Then trick yourself with the techniques in this chapter to get more accountability, reward, pain of failure and traction towards action without distraction.*

35
Environment & isolation

You've tidied up, set up a nice space to work in, planned your day, got your ducks in a row, had your drink of choice; you're just getting started and then BANG! - emails ping and ding and flood right in. The dog opens the door with his nose and the kids run in tearing the place to shreds. Your social media messages and notifications go into overdrive-spam mode. Everyone in China phones you at the same time. Five hours later having chased your tail for half a day, all dazed and confused, you forgot what, where and why you even started in the first place.

You can't blame the world for interrupting you. Any inbound communication you get, you've given some kind of permission to. You taught people to call you when they want. You have all your notifications turned on. You make yourself available at the beck and call of your clients day and night. It is not their fault, you trained them well! But here's the good news, you can (re) train them even better. Follow this simple process to block all interruptions:

1 Turn all notifications off (especially the sounds)
2 Put your phone away (don't answer it; route calls to answerphone)
3 Isolate yourself from all distractions (unplug the internet if you're brave enough)
4 Create an environment conducive for deep work

Create a space at home, in the office or shared space, in a coffee shop, in the middle of a forest; wherever you like best, where you feel the energy suits you (some like quiet, some like busy background; up to you). Ensure there is natural light and good clear space. If you like music; put it on, with massive headphones that say 'fuck off I'm busy' when you look at someone. Or peace and quiet if that is what works for you.

Now don't panic about losing clients or missing emergencies if you turn off your devices and don't answer your phone. You are simply retraining them to call you or book in a meeting on your times and terms. They will soon get used to it. You could set up an auto reply message that states where, when and how to contact you (i.e. not now). If there are serious emergencies people will contact you eight times on each device, so don't worry you will know.

Many people struggle with politely batting people off from interrupting them. I used to be a real wimp in this area. Here are some smart little tips I learned:

1 Say yes, thank you, but not right now. How about later at X time?
2 Route them to someone else like a PA, VA or answering service
3 Don't let anyone know where you are so they can't find you
4 Give them your best 'fuck off face'. This is what my Mum calls it. She says I have a well refined and perfected 'fuck off face'. Like Medusa. One little look and goodbye!

Start Now sound bite

Set up an environment conducive to deep work where you feel inspired. Isolate yourself from all distractions and devices. Retrain the world to know when you are available, on your terms.

36
Fire yourself

You are often the cause of the biggest bottleneck that is stopping you getting your stuff done, or leveraging others to get your stuff done. Leveraging out tasks, projects and responsibilities is a good start, but if you don't get completely and utterly out of their way, nothing will ever get finished without you being involved. This is unscalable and unsustainable but, secretly, you might like it, you kinky devil you. Let me explain:

1 You want control of the results and outcome
2 You want the task done exactly your way
3 You are a perfectionist and no one lives up to your (impossible) standards
4 You've hired people or asked them to do stuff before and they messed up
5 If you want a job done well, do it yourself
6 You want to feel all important and wanted

STOP.
These are all lies.

1. You want control of the results and outcome

Let go to grow. Set the goal, then let go. Get out of their way and let them do it their way. And who knows, they may do it better.

2. You want the task done exactly your way

Then either do it yourself, or let it go. Let them do it their way, under your guidance and guidelines, and they will own it, love it and may even produce something better.

3. You are a perfectionist and no one lives up to your (impossible) standards

Perfection is unattainable. Sure, strive for it, then settle for excellence. Then improve. If you judge and measure people by your own standards you will be perennially disappointed.

4. You've hired people or asked them to do stuff before and they messed up

Maybe you didn't train them well? Maybe you didn't give them the resources, support, confidence and autonomy needed to do great work? Even if it was their fault (which it rarely is), why stop looking? Find someone better or get better.

5. If you want a job done well, do it yourself

No. It is your responsibility to get people to care as much as you with respect and culture.

6. You want to feel all important and wanted

Get a puppy. At least you'll have time to play with it!

My friend Neville Wright sold his business that he loved, Kiddicare, for £70 million. The management company he hired to help with the sale told him to go away on holiday through the entire sales process. If he was seen in the building, the prospective buyers might feel he is needed operationally in the business, which devalues it. So, in effect, they fired him (so he could collect his share of the £70 million). The buyers want to buy a business that doesn't rely on any people, and most businesses are solely dependent on the grind and knowledge of the founder.

I edited my last book *Money* five full times. My publishers asked me to edit it down from 165,000 words to 120,000 words. After five full read throughs and hardcore editing, I got it down from 165,000 words to 165,000 words. Boom. Look at me! 5,000 words in, 5,000 words out, on each painstaking edit. Genius.

I. Was. The. Problem.

I needed to fire myself. Fast.

I kicked and screamed that the editors wouldn't know how to edit the book as well as me, after all it's my baby. When in fact they would (and did) edit it FAR better than me. Why have a publisher and edit yourself? And the good news is that you can take credit for the parts people love, and the parts they don't you can blame the publishers! Mwahaha. I wonder if they will edit this part out?

Start Now sound bite

Fire yourself fast. You are the problem. Get out of the way. Let go to grow. Trust others to do a good, or even better, job. If you are the bottleneck you will never scale.

37
If you want something done…

…Do. Not. Do. It. Yourself
(or as my Dad says: Destroy. It. Yourself). Instead…give it to a busy person!

It could be said Thomas Edison was a busy chap, yet he still managed to file over 1,000 patents. It took him around 10,000 experiments to figure out the lightbulb. Shunpei Yamazaki had 4,987 patents by 2017 and was still going strong.

Do not subscribe to the old view of: Do. It. Yourself. Or the slightly newer version: Destroy. It. Yourself. You need to change your pre-programmed 'hard work' upbringing into 'smart work'. You can trigger this change simply by asking better questions. Stop asking 'how' questions:

☐ How can I do it?
☐ How can I even get started doing it?

And change them to 'who' questions:

☐ Who can I get to do it?
☐ Who has vast experience doing it?
☐ For whom is it really easy?
☐ Who would love to do it (weirdo)?
☐ Who's already done it? (that I can copy, borrow from, leverage or partner with)

You might even want to note these down somewhere and have easy access to them so you can stop your old questions and start asking better ones. The quality of your life can be down to the quality of your questions.

Did you know that Thomas Edison didn't, in fact, do the 10,000 experiments himself. He set up Menlo Park research laboratory, and had smart people helping him with his experiments. So, in fact, he 'leveraged' the 10,000 experiments to achieve an outcome he may not have reached alone. That's the 'lightbulb'.

Start Now sound bite

If you want something done, find someone faster or better to do it. Even someone who loves it. Change your 'how' questions ('how can I do this?') to 'who' questions ('who can I get to do this?'). The quality of your questions can impact positively the quality of your life.

38
Carrot & stick

We are funny creatures. We are hard-wired to move towards pleasure and away from pain, and our brain gives us little chemical rewards and punishments to help us survive and thrive. A problem is that the world has changed so fast that many of the 'carrot and stick' feelings we now get, while useful for survival thousands of years ago, are outdated and confusing (like fearing public speaking worse than death).

Your vices are fighting against your virtues.

Your addictions are fighting against your visions. Your heart is fighting against your head. You're fighting what you feel you should do with what others tell you that you should do. You're trying to delay gratification for a better tomorrow, yet this fights against your survival instinct of the immediate danger today (so that you can actually get to tomorrow). You could call this discipline, which could be defined as: 'doing what you know you should be doing even when you don't feel like it'.

Here are a few simple steps you can take to improve your discipline, fight your natural urges of 'carrot and stick' and achieve maximum productivity with ruthless efficiency:

1. Give yourself rewards along the way, not all at the end

Micro-reward yourself with little breaks, procrastination after deep work and gifts or experiences to feed the internal beast of distraction (my inner bas-tard). Start small and scale up. Match the size of the reward to the size of the outcome.

2. Work out your strongest pleasure and pain motivations

Then leverage them and game yourself. What motivates you the most? What do you fear and hate? What would you most love to do, be and have? List them out, then use them against yourself to drive you away from your deepest fears and towards your greatest fantasies and legacies.

3. Have a very clear picture of your vision and goals

The clearer your goal, the easier it is to build up the picture piece by piece. You will never arrive at a destination you do not set, and it will take decades to get nowhere.

Start Now sound bite

Know what motivates you to the attainment of pleasure and the moving away from pain. Your vices are fighting against your virtues. Play them off against each other to motivate you to be disciplined by doing what you know you must do even when you don't feel like it.

39
FOMO

FOMO is the fear of missing out. Strong in you, it is. A be-yatch, it can be.

You are very susceptible to making bad decisions if you have FOMO, because you can't do everything and, therefore, most things you should *not* be doing. But you look from afar, with rose tinted glasses on, to the green, green grass over there and you can't help but think they've got it easier, faster, better and luckier. Let it be made official here: this is *not*, and *never* is, the reality. Every choice has an equal and opposite action and reaction, benefit and cost, upside and downside. FOMO often manifests itself by:

☐ Making you try to be everything to everyone
☐ Driving decisions based on competitiveness rather than vision
☐ Driving decisions based on low self-worth and/or comparison to others
☐ Driving decisions based on envy, revenge and ego
☐ Driving decisions without research or logic
☐ Driving decisions based on the crowd
☐ Creating unrealistic expectations (thinking it will be faster, better, easier)
☐ Getting you into things you don't understand
☐ Getting you into things you don't really want to do or will give up easily on
☐ Not allowing you clarity of your vision and goals

☐ Driving you to idolize someone else
☐ Making you either too excited or too downbeat
☐ Making you impatient and limited by a short-term focus

If you allow FOMO to rule your life, you will decision-hop from one thing to another to another, never sticking at it long enough for the acorn to grow into an oak tree. The more you do this, the more your self-worth will diminish as you will start to question why you can't achieve anything. When you are emotionally volatile like this, cycling from excitement to downtrodden, the sad irony is that you become even more susceptible to 'get rich quick' schemes and unrealistic promises or expectations. And, as such, repeat the very pattern you are trying to get out of.

Making a decision to do something just because you don't want to miss out on it can be the wrong basis on which to act. Every action has an equal and opposite reaction and, as such, the new shiny thing you jump into will take time, energy and results away from the thing you are already doing. There. Is. Always. A. Cost. Perhaps instead of the fear of missing out, you should also equally fear missing in. That is to say if you jump like a frog onto the next thing, you miss the results in the thing you are already doing, in which you are closer to achieving results as you have been doing it longer.

You wouldn't start drilling for oil, get one fifth of the way down, then give up, start again and drill one fifth of the way down the next oil well, and the next one and the next one and so on. This would be somewhat insane.

You wouldn't plant a seed today and come back annoyed tomorrow declaring, 'Well where's my fucking tree?'

One fifth of the way down five separate oil wells could be five fifths of the way down one oil well. And, revelation: you only get oil when you get all the way down. You only get your tree when the seed has grown deep roots, then shoots, then fruits. The grass is greener where you water it and give it sunlight.

A good way to overcome the FOMO beast is to observe the emotion, and then simply wait. Sure, that might be like saying sit and look at a drink for hours if you are an alcoholic, but try it. Just wait. Sit on your hands. Wait long enough for the extreme emotion to pass, and then allow yourself to evaluate the decision in a more balanced way.

Whenever you are making a decision make sure you balance the process by looking at the cost, not just the opportunity. Make sure you are not forcing it. If the thing you are missing out on is meant to be, it will come back to you. Sometimes doing the right thing at the wrong time is actually the *wrong* thing. Learn to say 'Yes, but not now'. Keep the door open, but just ajar. Make sure you can look yourself in the eye and be confident you gave the last thing long enough to bear fruit, before you move onto the next thing.

Look at your recurring FOMO patterns and blind spots. Each time you feel the strong urge, notice it. The more you notice it, and wait to let it subside, the more you master the beast.

Start Now sound bite

Fear of missing out (FOMO) is a strong emotion linked to low self-worth, lack of clarity and impatience. It will damage all progress and success, because you can't go one fifth of the way down five oil wells and strike oil in any of them. No grass is green except the grass you water, and every decision has equal benefit and cost. When you feel the FOMO is strong in you, notice it, and simply wait and allow it to pass. Then you can view the decision with balance and experience.

Research. Test. Review. Tweak. Repeat. (Scale.)

This section goes through my six-step process for making faster, better and bigger decisions, with lower risk. When I say mine, of course I mean one refined from testing myself, and also through mentors and the models I've learned, improving upon mistakes I've made in the past, so you don't have to make them as much.

Research (75%). Test. Review. Tweak. Repeat. (Scale.)

This simple six-step process will help you overcome inaction and procrastination, get more done quicker, making fewer mistakes and improving each time you repeat an action:

1. Research (75%)

Learn, prepare and do your diligence up front. Do not risk big, costly mistakes trying things yourself without knowledge and experience. But you will never have everything you need to de-risk every eventuality, so get about 75% of the knowledge you can to 'be ready,' to stop over-analysis and 'Start Now'.

2. Test

'Test' is better than 'do' because it assumes less risk, less permanence and a mindset of constant improvement. Get your MVP (Minimum Viable Product) out fast, and not perfect. It either works or you learn to make version two better. It's unlikely to be right the first time, so test it first and fast and improve as you go.

3. Review

Analyse and get feedback on your first test. What did you do well that you can keep doing? What do you need to start doing that you didn't do? What do you need to stop doing that isn't working? What do you need to keep?

4. Tweak

Tweak the first, next or most recent action for improvements. Make small, steady and constant improvements rather than slow, radical ones. This makes progress easier and less overwhelming for you and your end users.

5. Repeat

Loop back and start the process again, testing once more with improved skill, experience and confidence. If every action is seen as a test, it stops overwhelm, but also overconfidence. Each cycle you scale up little by little, improving the systems as you go; which prepares you for scale and sustainability.

6. Scale

After a series of loops from steps one through to five, you are ready to scale up. Don't scale up too quickly, or too slowly. Each cycle builds experience, security and systems that create the foundations for scale. This process is never done, so don't rest overconfidently that you've ever mastered it. Repeat the process for constant and never-ending improvement.

Detach yourself and your feelings from the outcome and result. Enjoy the journey and follow the process for more balanced emotions and long-term, sustainable success. It, and you, are never done. There's always more to learn and achieve. Strive for perfection but settle for excellence. Keep on keeping on towards your long-term vision.

SECTION 6.1: RESEARCH (75% 'READY')

You can never be 100% ready before you start. You will never have all your ducks in a row. Even if you did, someone will either move one of them out of line or shoot all of them off the wall. *To keep going, you have to get going.* Preparation prevents poor performance, but it can also keep you stuck in the planning stage. This one goes out to all the planners, procrastinators and perfectionists out there to help you overcome the disease of 'death by due diligence'. You are not alone...

40
Intuition vs. information

The balancing of intuition and information is the dance between research and action. When you start out, you need more information to build your intuition. The more experience you have, the more your intuition will guide you, which is the collated past experiences forward-informing you of upsides and downsides in the current situation.

It is said that your 'heart' or 'gut' is intuition, and your 'head' is information. Whichever way you break it down (be it logical and emotional, material and spiritual), it is wise to balance both and understand how each serves you (and can hinder you).

Intuition is good for:

1 Things you know; areas of existing experience
2 Relationships and partnerships that require more trust and discretion
3 People-related situations and those with high care requirements
4 Moral dilemmas and inner conflicts

Information is good for:

1 Data and analytical situations
2 Any areas of (modern) complexity or technology
3 Automation
4 Monetary, business and economic situations
5 Binary scenarios (A or B choice)

Intuition, the journey of 'following your heart', aids decision making by 'listening' to your feelings, both honouring and trusting your 'gut instinct'. After all, you have all your life experience up to this point, rolling forward into this feeling. You can also ask yourself these questions to help you trust your intuition:

☐ Does it feel right (even if I can't explain why)
☐ Will I be able to look myself in the mirror the next day?
☐ Will I be proud and happy about this decision in the future?
☐ Who could this affect?

Even without these questions, we all know the single spontaneous right action (SRA). Intuition is about trusting yourself, having the courage to make the right (but not necessarily easiest) decision, and being patient that the right outcome will materialize. If you find that you have to talk yourself into something, it is usually the wrong decision.

If you found a wallet on the floor with money in it, you know the right thing to do would be to...

...give it to me. Ha, only kidding. Of course, you'd hand it in. If you saw a lost child, would you stop to help? You'll be placed with situations and moral dilemmas frequently. Making the right call makes them easier in the future as they build on each other.

Information (that you research) is about data, facts, split-tests, due-diligence and measurable past experience. Brian Tracy said that, 'one minute planning saves five minutes of doing (and probably 10 minutes of mistakes)'.

When gathering data before making a decision, go the extra mile in collecting all available information, *with a set deadline*. A frequent problem with decision making is that some people gather only the data that's quickly available, on the surface or, worse, supports their favourite choice or confirmation bias (result they want). Target getting approximately 75% of the data, set a clear outcome, and research what you think you need to be perfectly ready. Then you must hit the trigger: decide and act.

This research can include getting good counsel from those with vast experience. Tim Ferriss (author of *The 4-Hour Work-week*), is a good modern-day example of someone who has interviewed many smart people to both improve his own life, and help others by repackaging that information into podcasts and books. I get to learn so many things interviewing the greats with vast experience on my podcast, the 'Disruptive Entrepreneur'.

The paradox for the anal-yst is many of these research 'deep dives' end up all-consuming, sucking them into the trap of procrastination. Get wise counsel, but not from too many people. Get variant options, but perhaps only look at three or four alternatives (i.e. not one, and not 101). Give yourself some time, but not too much time. There is an abundance of research that shows that when people look thoroughly at three or more alternatives, a better option typically emerges. Too many and you get sucked into the paradox of choice, where overwhelm causes you to pick none.

Get to the deadline and then JFDI.

Start Now sound bite

Use both intuition and information to make informed decisions. Know when to use one or other, or both. You know the single right action when following your heart but must research when following your head. Set a clear outcome of about 75% of the perfect research you could do, give yourself enough time but a hard deadline, then decide and act.

41
De-risk the downside

Risk is a delicate balance. Undue risks can lead to unnecessary mistakes or, worse, losing it all. But *if you don't risk anything, you risk everything.* Risk and reward are two parts of the same whole, where reduced risk usually leads to a more secure but lower return, and bigger risks can lead to bigger rewards but also an epic fail. It's important to embrace the risk-reward relationship, and not take a one-sided view of risk. If you are strategic, you can manage risk progressively by sticking to the following principles:

1 Start with safer, more proven, lower risk models or investments
2 Build up your risk experience and threshold progressively
3 As you increase risk, reduce exposure
4 Know when you're gambling and only risk money you can afford to lose
5 Learn as well as earn; increased risk gives increased lessons
6 Protect the downside as much as you can

Richard Branson might look like a fun-loving, hair-flowing, fancy-free risk taker, but he's famous for protecting the downside risk first. It's this that *enables* him to be more fun-loving. He approached Boeing and negotiated to buy their aircraft on the condition that if the airline fails, Boeing will take the aircraft back from him. Boeing agreed because they wanted someone to compete with British Airways. This meant his worst-case scenario was de-risked to the start-up and lost profit costs, but not the huge overhead of aircraft he couldn't do anything with, which was by far the biggest expense. This then sets up the best-case scenario: a successful business that could generate hundreds of millions. You know the ending to this story.

A risk is a well-calculated and researched investment decision, where as much downside has been protected (as is possible). Then an initial amount of time or money is invested, then progressively increased as results show or tweaks and improvements are made. As you gain great exposure, you now have a paradoxical risk of too much in one place (that becomes vulnerable due to your over-reliance on it). You then de-risk by diversifying and reducing exposure in certain classes or models. And you take forward all the lessons and experience you gain along the way to feed that forward into smarter, faster decision making.

A gamble is a blind decision based on extreme emotion with time and money you cannot afford to lose in a hope that you will get a big (lucky) win. And it gets highly addictive; feeding itself to get worse and worse, because the odds are always stacked in favour of the house.

Know the difference. Protect the downside with good research and diligence, reducing costs and exposure, having break clauses and option agreements, insurances, plan Bs and other protective mechanisms.

Start Now sound bite

De-risk and protect the downside so that you can go all in to get the upside.

42

'What's the worst that could (really) happen?'…& other good questions

People often take their worries, fears and 'what ifs' too seriously, or out of context. Our brains are 'designed' to take fear more seriously than positive emotions and, as such, we worry too much about what could happen (just in case it does), instead of what is likely to happen.

In the modern Western world, we are unlikely to have our village looted and entire tribe murdered if we venture out. It is wise to manage your fears because many of them are thousands of years out of date. We've already covered contextualizing the decision, safe in the knowledge that we don't have the responsibility of people dying, no matter what decision we make. Once we realize we are making the decision much bigger *in our own minds*, then these exercises should further ease the weight, responsibility and, therefore, procrastination and overwhelm:

1. Ask yourself 'What's the worst that can happen?'

Satisfy yourself that you won't die. Then that you aren't in real danger. Then contextualize the situation, knowing what the worst-case scenario *really* is.

2. Worst-case, likely-case and best-case scenario planning

Plan out these three scenarios for your impending decision to help you be proactive (whilst allaying your concerns):

WORST-CASE

Death and public humiliation unlikely. Check. If you are think-ing about leaving your job to start your own business, it is highly likely the worst case is you'll have to go back to a job. At worse you might have to take a 20% pay cut. You may be a little humbled. But you aren't likely to die of rabies slowly. At least you tried to answer your calling and now have more clar-ity on what you should be doing. You also have more knowl-edge and experience. *It's better to regret something you have done, than something you haven't,* though you likely won't regret most things you try because at least you will know, even if it didn't go your way.

LIKELY-CASE

You'll probably make some mistakes. It may take longer than you thought or be a struggle at times. That's normal. If you keep going, you'll get better and in time you'll get good. *You earn or you learn, you keep going and you keep growing.*

BEST-CASE

You could gain freedom, choice and profit. You could make millions *and* make a difference. You could be a wild success and leave a vast and lasting legacy. You could also find new hori-zons you never even thought (or dreamed) of. Well, you'll never know unless you try.

3. Parallel universe thinking

Plot out the most likely scenarios as if you get to do them both/all in a parallel universe. What is likely to happen in Scenario A, Scenario B, and so on? Trick your mind into thinking you are testing these scenarios. This simple technique will give you more clarity on the options you face and build up your self-awareness as you project forward; getting better at predicting how you will think, feel, react and decide.

Here are some other questions that can help you 'Start Now. Get Perfect Later':

1 What is the most important thing I need to do right now (not urgent)?
2 What is the one thing that would negate the need to do everything else?
3 Should I be doing this task at all (L1 M2 DL – see Chapter 30)?
4 What are my highest (non-negotiable) priorities?
5 What resources do I need to make it easy to get started?
6 Based on past experience, what usually happens to stop me from taking action?
7 What do I need to STOP doing?
8 What would [insert committed person/mentor] do?

Start Now sound bite

Satisfy yourself that your worst fears are unlikely to happen. Then plot out worst-case, likely-case and best-case scenarios. Imagine a parallel universe of outcomes, so that you can protect the downside risk and allay your concerns to forge forward with conviction. Use the list of eight questions above to give you clarity of next, right action.

43
Pros & Cons

One of the most simple, yet effective, ways to banish procrastination and overwhelm is to get all the noise out of your head
and onto paper (or screen) in front of you. It's hard to actually
see it inside your confused mind but much clearer on a sheet
with a line down the middle.

When evaluating or procrastinating, put 'Pro' or 'Upside' on
the left-hand side, and 'Con' or 'Downside' on the right-hand
side. List them all out. The decision will likely make itself for
you as you brain dump; you'll simply see it manifest before
your eyes.

This simple, yet powerful, exercise can be done on a Post-It
Note for a simple decision, or on a larger sheet in more detail
for a complex decision. It can also be done for the following:

1 Partnerships and joint ventures
2 To apportion and delineate roles and responsibilities
3 For hiring and creating roles and job descriptions
4 Heads of terms and contracts
5 Big decisions or areas you are putting off for extended
  periods
6 Which school to send your kids to
7 Which house or neighbourhood to move into
8 Weighing up career options
9 General brainstorming and ideation

Start Now sound bite

Do not underestimate the power of the simple 'Pros' and 'Cons', 'Upsides' and 'Downsides' listing exercise. Stop thinking, start writing. The answer will likely unfold in front of your eyes. If in doubt, get it out.

44
Opportunity cost decision making

No decision or action has all upside or all downside. This is important to embrace because, by our nature, we get clouded by extremes. It is hard to maintain balance when something seems so bad (or so good) because, in that moment, all we can feel is the single overriding emotion. It's rare to feel both a positive and negative emotion simultaneously. Wisdom and sustainability come from being able to see the balanced, entire picture. That means seeing the potential downside risks when you're flying high and seeing the upside lessons when you're facing challenges. I tend to see more upside which makes me occasionally naive or unrealistic, and my wife tends to see more downside which makes her...

...right.

When making your choices, what's important is not just knowing the decision making, but the 'opportunity cost' of where that decision is moving you away from. Consider when making a decision:

☐ What will you *not* be able to now do?
☐ What will you have to sacrifice, let go or give up?
☐ How much time, money, reward and energy will the decision cost?

The opportunity cost of buying a car with cash is the return that cash could get in an investment, so consider a lease deal too. The opportunity cost of staying in a job you dislike for a decade is the time, freedom and uncapped income you could get working for yourself. In more detailed or complex decisions, opportunity cost can be less obvious. Here are some examples to help you calculate opportunity cost:

1 Time in one thing takes time away from another thing
2 How much time and energy will the decision take or drain from you?
3 One too many things could break all things
4 Could the decision reduce your time value (IGT)? (Is it even worth your time?)
5 Spent/invested money could get an alternative (better) return somewhere else...

...and so it is with time, energy, creativity, resourcefulness, drive, passion and enthusiasm.

Working overtime might make more money, but the cost might be your relationship with your kids. Having a few drinks might be fun but the opportunity cost could be a three-day hangover. A 'debate' on social media might look tempting but it could cost your entire weekend! Be self-aware by seeing both the opportunity and the cost.

Start Now sound bite

Your decisions and actions have an opportunity cost, in that they can block and prevent you investing time, money and energy into other things that could be more productive. Consider not just what you are about to do, but the cost of doing it. There is always a cost, and wisdom comes from seeing the upside in the downside and the downside in the upside.

SECTION 6.2

Test

When all is said and done, more is said than done.

Most of us know what we need to do, but to know and not to do is not to know.

You do and you learn. You wait and you stagnate.

If you stop seeing decisions as final and start seeing all decisions as a series of tests that can be tweaked and adjusted *as* you go, not *before* you go, then you will be in flow. A big decision is a series of small decisions anyway, so you need to start making the smaller ones to lead to the bigger outcomes. As you go the decision will need to change along the journey anyway, including some improvements you didn't know in advance that you needed to make. Tests embrace improvement and iteration.

Decisions that seem to need to be final create pressure and stress. But, in reality, no decision is final. Paradoxically, the more 'final' a decision is perceived or made, the harder it is to change. So stop thinking of any decision as final because then you take away the pressure, which relaxes you into better decision making.

If in doubt, test.

If you're on the fence, test.

Even if you're sure, test; because then you stay open minded to a better outcome.

Failure is discouraged with more final decisions, whereas it is embraced as part of the progressive improvement with testing. Test a new holiday destination with a short stay first. Test a new date but get your mate to wait outside in the car just in case. Test a new restaurant or a different meal on the menu; go on, I dare you!

Coca-Cola would not have gone from medicinal to refreshment purposes without staying open to test results and feedback. Lamborghini wouldn't have gone from tractors to cars. In fact, Nintendo went from producing playing cards to vacuum cleaners to instant rice to a taxi company and even a short-stay hotel chain. Those changes, viewed as open-minded tests, helped them all pivot into the world-leading businesses they are today.

45
(How to) Start Now. Get Perfect Later.

GOYA and JFDI.

Get off your arse (ass) and just fuckin' (frickin') do it.*

You now have most of the strategies and tactics to make good, fast, smart decisions. What more do you need? Whilst you now know that perfection is unattainable, you will never get anywhere near it doing nothing. Don't let the desire for perfection get in the way of excellence, or simply making small baby steps of progress.

Your decisions and actions are so unlikely to be best first time around. You might even look back thinking they were pretty bad, compared to where you are now. You only get better (or perfect) later, so why not get your first decision out of the way, so you can get to your next better one as soon as you can?

And no one will remember your first decision anyway.

Doing something mostly beats doing nothing.

It's never too late to start, but it's always too late to wait.

Talk less, do more. Or from the famous Chinese proverb *'talk doesn't cook rice'*.

☐ What you *can* change: change it.
☐ What you *can't* change: leave it.
☐ What you *do* change: live it.

No decision needs to be permanent. Any decision can be changed or improved, quickly. See every decision as a test which

---

* Did you guess what these were, or did you do a cheeky Google search?

reduces the risk and develops a mindset of constant improvement. Get your MVP, 'good enough' decision out fast, not perfect. It either works, or you learn to make it better. Then repeat over and over. Big decisions are made up of many progressive smaller decisions.

Nike's tagline is 'Just Do It', not 'Nah, Fuck It'.

When I started in property I had just one house and no deposits for any more. I had no experience or credibility to view and make offers on properties. The estate agents probably thought I was a clown. But one property led to two led to 20, 50, 500 and more. I'm getting perfect later all the time.

When I wrote my first book it was average, at best. But my book *done* was better than my book perfect (but never done). That average first book (in my opinion, because Mum and a few others loved it) is now on its fourth edition, and the best-selling property book in the UK. If it weren't for the imperfect version one, there would be no (significantly) better version four.

You should have seen my first website. In fact, I'm glad you didn't! I looked about 15 and sounded like a robot. But it was better than not having one and not being found.

You would have been embarrassed *for me* at my first public speech. Cringe. I read from pages of crumpled notes and stood in front of the projector so you had to read the slides from my crotch area. I am by no means the finished article now but, over 1,200 speeches later and a five-figure speaking fee, I'm getting perfect later.

Warning: don't be flippant and put rubbish out into the world, or be lazy or apathetic with your decisions. Some professions (such as medical, security and safety professions) require perfect processes, otherwise someone could die. Don't 'get perfect later' performing surgery or starting-up your passenger airline! In situations where serious consequences or death could happen, don't be flippant with 'get perfect later', do it right first time.

Start Now sound bite

GOYA and JFDI. 'Start Now. Get Perfect Later'. No decision is final, so see all decisions as tests that can be changed quickly and that give you steady progress towards your goal.

46

Experience, but not too much

Experience has its obvious benefits: wisdom, intuition and confidence. But it has drawbacks that many people are oblivious to.

So many people just won't start anything until they feel they have all the confidence and experience which, of course, is a paradox because you only get the confidence and experience by starting.

Sometimes with experience also comes:

1 A hardened attitude
2 Diminished passion and enthusiasm, fatigue or, worse, full burn-out
3 Cynicism and a lack of trust
4 A lack of energy
5 A lack of creativity and resourcefulness due to always doing it the same way
6 Boredom and becoming stuck in a rut
7 Over-confidence, arrogance or hubris
8 A lack of effort and care, or taking things for granted

You will not have (m)any of these when you start out or start a new, big decision. You don't have the luxury. You don't have the results yet. You don't have the fatigue. Leverage this paradoxical asset in your favour, by seeing and focusing on the latent assets within you, as this balances experience.

I bet there was a day when you hadn't had any experience in sex, but you gave it a damn good go anyway and relied on other assets than experience!

You often hear those with hardened, fatigued experience say, 'If I'd have known then what I know now I'd never have started'. Then it's a damn good job you don't have all the experience up front. There's a certain amount of naivety required to go into big, unproven decisions. Never lose that naivety. Never lose your youthful positivity, belief, creativity and resourcefulness. It keeps you young, humble and open-minded. Balance this with the experience you gain along the way and leverage the experience of others, and you win all ways.

Start Now sound bite

By all means use the experience you have, but not too much. You also need youthful naivety, creativity and resourcefulness. Be careful not to get too hardened and lose your passion and enthusiasm. Equally balance your experience, that of others ahead of you and positive open-mindedness.

47
Change your mind

Many people see changing their mind as a weakness. Somehow, they feel it will undermine their initial decision. They hold on to bad decisions, making them worse and becoming more stubborn and inflexible for no good reason (other than to protect their ego or the need to be right). Therefore, they make a bad decision worse, or block a better decision coming their way.

Changing your mind (as long as it isn't every five seconds) is a strength, not a weakness. It shows you don't hold onto the past, and you can separate your ego from your decision making. It shows you can adapt to changes. The only constant is change anyway, so the skill of changing your mind, or improving decisions progressively, is a prerequisite for achieving results.

'To improve is to change; to be perfect is to change often'

Winston Churchill

Three words I could never say were 'I was wrong'. It was like I was Robocop and my programming protocol just couldn't say the words. I'd hold onto and defend decisions from years previous that were clearly wrong, just for the sake of protecting my fragile ego. In reality, no one cared and telling people 'I was wrong' actually allows them to feel important and builds rapport between you.

'I was wrong. You were right. Thank you. Sorry.'

If you want a lasting, happy marriage, use these four magic phrases often.

'I was wrong. You were right. Thank you. Sorry.'

If you want happy staff, customers, followers and fans, use these magic phrases often. One at a time, or all at once if you've made a clear and massive balls up.

'I was wrong. You were right. Thank you. Sorry.'

Blockbuster held onto high street video rentals for far too long. They were given a few opportunities to purchase Netflix for $50 million in the early 2000s. They decided an inferior brand was beneath them, which ultimately led to their demise and, by 2017, Netflix had risen in value to $70 billion.

> **Start Now sound bite**
>
> *As long as you don't change your mind all the time for no good reason, changing your mind when it is right to do so is a strength, not a weakness. Give people power by saying 'I was wrong' if you need to, and separate changing your mind from your protective ego. 'I was wrong. You were right. Thank you. Sorry.'*

48
The law of proportional decision making

The law of proportional decision making states that 'the amount of time invested into making a decision should be directly proportional to its outcomes'. Big decisions with big outcomes require (and should be given) more time. Smaller decisions with smaller outcomes require (and should be given) much less time.

You already do this automatically with habitual, mundane tasks like brushing your teeth. Which means you can apply this law to smaller tasks which you may give too much weight to. You then conserve your energy and decision fatigue for more important tasks and decisions. *No two tasks have the same value* but people tend to repeat their habits and, as such, make very quick or very slow decisions most of the time. This goes against this law and will not serve you well.

Ask yourself at the start of a decision how important this is. You could even rank it one to five,* as a quick check in to see how much time, planning, research and counsel you should invest into the decision. If the scale is at one, you could make the decision very quickly. Even better you could outsource the decision quickly to someone else. This frees time to invest into a decision that is four or five on the scale, in which case time invested into planning and research will pay off.

---

* Rank it one to five. Don't take seven years to work out what score between one and five your decision is on the scale. I'm watching you!

Carry forward your knowledge of decision fatigue, intuition vs. information, de-risking the downside and Pros and Cons to the Law of Proportional Decision Making.

Start Now sound bite

The law of proportional decision making states that the amount of time invested into a decision should be proportional to its size and importance. Use a one to five scale to measure the importance of your decision to help you know when to make fast and slow decisions, because no two decisions have the same time value.

49
Crowdsource it

If in doubt, leverage it out.

In nearly all cases of results and success, the way you get there and even what it ends up looking like, is different from how you planned, perceived or believed. *You can't solve those problems in advance because you don't know what they will be in advance.*

But imagine for a moment if you could work out what most of those problems (and solutions) would be, in advance. Might that make your journey towards success faster, easier and better? Imagine if you could 'outsource' decisions and reduce the risk of making the wrong ones.

Well you can, for the most part. It is called 'crowdsourcing'. Whilst this is mostly seen as a business function, it is highly relevant and applicable to your personal life too. According to Dictionary.com, crowdsourcing is 'the practice of obtaining information or input into a task or project by enlisting the services of a large number of people, either paid or unpaid, typically via the Internet'.

If you want to de-risk watching a dodgy film, you might ask your friends on social media or read peer reviews. The same goes for choosing a restaurant or holiday destination. You are simply pooling other people's previous experience to reduce the time and energy to make a decision, and the risk of making a bad one.

The hardest way to solve problems, progress and make more money is to come up with all the ideas yourself. It can take great energy and risk, you can meet resistance and you may need to go into realms of your mind you've never been before. A *significantly* easier way is to get the ideas from friends, mentors, smart people and customers who buy what you sell or have done what you want. They've experienced the problem or the solution before.

In a business situation, once you have asked and received these ideas, you test the solutions back on the reviewers or users, monetizing those ideas through testing the suggestions. Microsoft has done this with virtually every version of Windows. Do this and you can proceed more confidently knowing that your idea will work, because you have both the ideas and the demand tested in advance.

The magic in crowdsourcing is that it can become part of the marketing or pre-sales process. If you have involved the users at development stage of a product or service then they have awareness of it *before* it is launched. This will nag away at them like seeing images of the new iPhone before it goes on sale. Tesla did it with their new Roadster a full three years before release. They know about it, have bought into it and 'own' a part of it in their mind.

It is less effort and risk to buy what you know you already want. You will tell others to buy it too, all before it is even ready. I have made this a part of all my book launches. First, I poll the concepts of three to five potential book ideas. I get enough data for it to be a relevant test and always go with the significant majority. I then put ideas out for the title, subtitle, the cover designs, and chapters I may need more research on. In addition to having a better, more thoroughly tested book, my readers know about the book well before launch. The book is far more likely to be what you want and you feel part of the creation of it. And you wait in anticipation of it.

You can run competitions to incentivize people further to help you, as well as give away prizes, do polls, run focus groups, give products for them to test, or simply ask for help.

If you feel you are not really creative or you like to model what works (and you want to reduce your risks), then crowdsourcing is the best answer you are likely to find. There is no real 'get rich quick', but the get rich in the most realistically quick time is crowdsourcing.

Start Now sound bite

If in doubt, leverage it out. Crowdsource your problems and solutions to your customers, followers, fans and community members. Ask them what they want, go with the majority, create it for them and keep improving and repeating the process.

Review. Tweak. Repeat. (Scale.)

Once you have tested or crowdsourced a product, service or idea, many people think the work is done. In fact, it has only just started. Version one is never as good as version two, and shouldn't be. The 'Review. Tweak. Repeat.' stages are as important as getting your work out to the world.

As you have some users, you also have some potential complainers if you do not listen to the feedback and make the necessary improvements. The process is simple: Review. Tweak. Repeat. Then after a few iterations of the testing loop. Scale.

Never scale too early, because you also scale your problems. So you may have three, five or more rounds of 'Review. Tweak. Repeat.' before you go to the wider market or do a full-scale launch. Here are some ways to effectively (and with least risk) go through the 'Review. Tweak. Repeat. Scale.' process:

Review

1. Good counsel

Ensure you get feedback and advice from people with experience, including users, mentors and staff who are in the department. If you don't have wise people to bounce ideas off, then they will rattle inside your head, creating more overwhelm.

2. Feedback

Ask. Shut up. Listen. Take note. Don't judge. Thank them. Make decision. Repeat.

3. Advice, but not too much

There is such a thing as too much advice or too many mentors. Don't get so much data that you get overwhelmed and do nothing.

4. Sleep on it, or take time out

Some decisions are bigger and need time to settle in your mind. You need to let extreme emotions subside, give the weight of the decision the proportional amount of time, and let your unconscious get to work and seek out the solutions.

5. KPIs

Key Performance Indicators, or data sets, have the answers hidden in plain sight. Always analyse the numbers and key metrics, and make decisions based on past experience and fact, as opposed to guesswork or biases.

Tweak

1. Process of iteration

An aircraft is off course up to 97% of the flight, constantly tweaking its course. Small and regular tweaks are mostly better than revolutionary, risky big changes.

2. Progressive improvements

Do not change everything or too much all at once. If you change just one isolated thing at a time, you know the impact of the variable. If you change everything, you don't know what worked and what didn't. Most people assume change equals improvement, but often changes break things. Small single changes are easier too.

3. Progressive automation

As you tweak and make iterative improvements, automate your tweaks so that you don't have to go back to them and keep fixing them. Update the system, keep progressing.

Repeat

Simply repeat the 'Review. Tweak.' process, implementing any improvements progressively. Keep a testing mentality by making sure you change small or singular things, not everything.

Scale

Only once you have good data, experience and have stress-tested systems, should you scale up. There is such a thing as scaling too fast, where you can break good things because you couldn't handle the capacity. It might be tempting when you get some good early results to go big, but that could be more dangerous than staying small. Ensure a few rounds of 'Review. Tweak. Repeat.' before you 'Scale'.

One final note. You need to know when to say no. Know when to abort or let go. Don't think you have to finish everything you start. In fact, flogging a dead horse can cost you significant money, time and reputation. This can be small things and big things. If a book you're reading isn't great, stop it and read something else. If your business or a product within it isn't working, stop it. Of course, you don't want to start everything and finish nothing. Conversely, get rid of your need for perfectionism or fear of judgement of having to finish everything if it isn't right. Don't let your fear of the consequences of stopping things (like having to let people go from their jobs or ending a bad relationship) stop you from making the right decision.

SECTION 7

How to make faster, better, harder decisions

As you make faster, better and harder decisions, you get better at making faster, better and harder decisions. *See every decision as an investment you carry over into the next decision.* What once was hard becomes easier over time.

This section carries forward all the strategies and tactics so far, to build your decision muscle and set you up for the progressively harder and more important decisions you will need to make. In addition to things getting easier as you get better, you also earn the right and open the door to harder and more critical decisions. Don't get ready, be ready. Come with me...

50
Rest & play (without guilt)

When I started my companies, I was single, hungry and skint. That makes for great motivation to 'hustle and grind'. I threw wayward energy all over the place at everything, but much of it was wasted or misdirected. I'd feel guilt and a decline in progress if I took any time off, even an hour a day, because my only measure of results was 'graft'. I would burn out once a year or so. It would usually result in me getting ill, as this seemed to be the only way to force me to stop and rest.

This cycle repeated for around four years and, whilst I became relatively successful (and a millionaire in that time), it was unsustainable. I was young and stubborn and wouldn't listen to people giving me advice to slow down, rest, or at least be patient, because I felt there was a long way to go yet. I felt I had lost time to make up for, for messing about for a quarter of a century and the only asset I knew, or had at the time, was graft, and not craft.

Feeling like an old bas-tard of 38 I now see what the older, wiser generation were telling me. Life is a marathon not a sprint. Of course, in the grand scheme of infinite time, life flashes by. With the average life expectancy now over 80, and rising, it is wise to think in that length of time, and ensure you stay fit, healthy and motivated for the full duration. If you do what you love and love what you do, you will likely merge your passion and profession well into your eighties.

Many musicians, artists, celebrities and sports stars, some of whom I know personally, have such intense and short careers they end up totally burning out. They can get lost, depressed, lose purpose and often don't have enough income to sustain the rest of their life. Warren Buffett was worth around 1% of his net worth by age 50. It was still a lot, but most of his compounded growth came in the nearly 40 years after. When asked about the key to his sustained success he quipped: 'Three things: living in America for the great opportunities, having good genes so I lived a long time, and compound interest.'

Whilst at first this can seem flippant, it has more depth the longer you consider it. We are in a paradoxical age where, on the one hand, millennials are being accused of being lazy and entitled, balanced with the American influencers telling people to hustle and that the only way to success is to grind it out 18 hours a day. The sustained balance is in the middle. Sure, work hard, deep and focused for intense yet short bursts of time, and then rest and play to allow you to:

1 Recover energy and emotional control
2 Allow ideas and creativity in
3 Ensure you don't delay what you want today
4 Stay radiant, charismatic and attractive
5 Live the longest, most meaningful life

This is also a note to self, because my default is to go hard-hard-hard. I was raised by a very hard-working entrepreneur, who didn't have the privilege and leverage of the Internet, social media, outsourcers and apps. Graft was the key asset a generation ago but leverage, reach, influence, creativity, problem solving, building teams and systems, strategy and vision are now all at least as equally valuable as hard graft.

Hard graft can push people away from you because you get stressed and flip out at them when they don't deserve it. Sometimes it's at people you love the most. You wouldn't do this if you were well 'played' and well 'rested'. This is not who you are, it is how you react when stressed or overwhelmed. You can also smell a little of desperation which, again, is unattractive. No one wants to be the date that broke a long dry spell for someone else. You have to look after yourself to attract others to you. Sure, achievement and ambition are part of this, but so is faith and belief and patience balanced with persistence.

Golfers have long careers. I know a couple of very successful golfers. They started at three or four years old. They are playing into their late 30s, even late 40s. How do they maintain such a long career without boredom or, worse, burn-out? Many don't if they overcook themselves. The ones that sustain will take significant periods of time completely off, and for two to four weeks they don't even touch a golf club. In many ways this must be hard for them, knowing they could gather some dust and fall back a few weeks against their competition. But, importantly, it keeps them hungry. If the hunger goes, so does all motivation. Sometimes you need time away, to rest and play, to build the hunger back up.

Between 26 and 31, I worked really hard. It wasn't really a problem to anyone else when I was single and skint. When I met my now wife, she accepted me for who I was and gave me the freedom to work hard and long. Then one day, at our favourite Thai restaurant over a panang curry, she uttered two words that changed my life:

'I'm pregnant.'

Around 18 months later she sat me down and in her elegant way said: 'Rob, I'm proud of what you've built, and love you for who you are, but if you keep working this hard, going to work before Bobby wakes and coming home after he goes to bed, your son will be 18 and you won't know who he is.'

This hit me hard. I was defensive at first, citing that all my hard work was for my family. But, in reality, it wasn't. It was because of fear and guilt and lack of long-term balance and wisdom. If you have read *Life Leverage*, (how to get more done in less time, outsource everything and create your ideal mobile lifestyle), then you have my wife to thank, because I went full out and made myself completely redundant from my businesses so she could never say this to me again. Work hard because you choose to, not because you have to.

Start Now sound bite

Work, rest and play. Stay hungry. Give yourself time to be creative, recover energy and emotions and stay radiant so you can maintain focus and enthusiasm for 80 to 100 years.

51
Clear-outs & cleanses

In order to balance work, rest and play, deep intense focus needs recovery time. Periodical clear-outs and cleanses of space and mind are important. Advanced warning: please do not use this as an excuse to procrastinate. 'Rob said clear your space and mind so I tidied up and meditated all day. Where's my £10million?' Er, no.

You could consider the following periodic strategies to clear your mind, body and space of all distraction and noise, so you can banish overwhelm and procrastination and get more done in less time. Remember that one minute in planning saves five minutes doing, and so it is with periodic, planned clear-outs and cleanses:

1 Remove all clutter from visible space:
   a Quick clear and tidy-ups
   b Occasional full-scale office and home clear-outs
2 Full diary cleanse once/twice a year (review, delete and rebuild appointments)
3 Device purge (emails, apps, folders, history); save, back up and clear all files
4 Clear your head (run, meditate, mindful exercise, rest):
   a Daily
   b Once/twice a year complete getaway, hideaway or holiday

5 'To do' lists/notes/ideas. (Weekly file away. Clear out. Move on. Store for later)
6 Regular health cleanses and check-ups
7 Forgive and let go of past mistakes and perceived wrongs of others

In *Money* I discussed the 'vacuum law of prosperity'. In order to attract more into your life, you need to free and clear the space to allow it. This goes for material items like periodic clear-outs of clothes and clutter to free up space for the new. This applies for money too: give in order to receive. Do not hoard. Start the flow to receive the flow. This applies to your mind too: in order to receive ideas, creativity and solutions, you must first empty your bursting brain. A full, cluttered mind has no space to allow ideas in. *You are infinitely creative, but only when there is free space.* In order to experience good emotions, you need to clear out the bad emotions you are holding onto. Make peace with your past mistakes, and the mistakes you perceive others made towards you. Both you and they did the best they could with what they knew at the time.

A good colonic will do it for your body too!*
Maybe you need to apply the 'vacuum law of prosperity' for some hanger-on-er or so-called friend, to allow better quality, more aligned people into your life.

Letting go of some of your past baggage will allow the great things you desire to come into your life. Deleting all your dating accounts and dropping all your back-up plan booty-calls will allow space for the person of your dreams to come into your life, at just the right time.

Just like a computer over-full of apps and folders slows down the processor and the speed (sometimes so much so you can

---

* Please don't get addicted to colonics as a method of active procrastination.

hear the whirring and feel the over-heating), so it is with any space in your life that you clog and clutter up. *Let go of the lesser to free up space for the greater.*

> ### Start Now sound bite
>
> *Periodic cleanses and clear-outs will free space in all areas of your life for the lesser to make way for the greater. Both frequently and occasionally, but deeply, clear out, cleanse and purge your body, mind, devices, distractions, regrets, baggage, emotions, finances and diary to come back free, open and energized.*

52
Getting in flow (with least effort)

As a reminder, Mihaly Csikszentmihalyi, author of *Flow*, calls the flow state 'an optimal state of intrinsic motivation, where the person is fully immersed in what they are doing'. The point here is not to repeat the earlier chapter, but to add to it. In addition to maximizing time and minimizing effort and resistance, it is easier to make harder and more important decisions when you are in a state of flow (or zone, or groove). You will naturally trust your intuition more, and ideas and solutions will flow to you and through you.

Sometimes people push too hard, think too much and stress themselves out over hard and important decisions. That may even be the understatement of the century. This is understandable because of the law of proportional decision making and the weight of big decisions. Paradoxically, trying harder and harder often results in a worse outcome.

Bruce Lee gained all his power in his technique from being relaxed, not tense, trying less hard with kicks and punches. Power in the cue action of snooker players comes from a very relaxed grip. Great comedians seem relaxed and natural. Cricketers hit fours and sixes from timing over brute strength. In all areas of what seems like effortless finesse and skill, a state of 'least effort' and relaxation is key. Of course, it took much effort and practice to get to this place and state.

'Practice like it's a competition so you can compete like it's a practice session'

Bob Rotella

In Deepak Chopra's 7 *Laws of Spiritual Success*, one of his laws is the 'Law of Least Effort'. I've tried so damn hard to get this law to work! The harder I try...

One of my flaws is that sometimes I can push too hard. This can be in sport, where you often need to stay relaxed, or sometimes defaulting to a work hard–hard–hard, instead of a work smart mindset and skillset. Sometimes I am too persistent that I can annoy people. Sometimes you have to let them come to you. Sometimes you have to let go to grow. Chopra states that:

'Nature's intelligence functions with effortless ease, with carefreeness, harmony, and love. This is the principle of "Do less, and accomplish more". When we learn this lesson from nature, we easily fulfil our desires. Grass doesn't try to grow; it just grows. Fish don't try to swim; they just swim. This is their intrinsic nature. It is the nature of the sun to shine. And it is human nature to make our dreams manifest into physical form – easily and effortlessly.

'When we seek power and control over other people, we spend energy in a wasteful way. When we seek money for personal gain only, we cut off the flow of energy to ourselves, and interfere with the expression of nature's intelligence. We waste our energy chasing the illusion of happiness, instead of enjoying happiness in the moment.'

I find this a very powerful concept that sometimes we have to get out of the way. Sometimes we have to force it less. It is *us* that blocks nature's natural order. Set a goal, work towards it of course, but don't push too hard. Don't try to over-control how your kids behave. How your staff perform their projects.

How people measure up to your expectations. Have faith in the infinite intelligence, or whatever the 'higher order' is to you. To experience the 'Law of Least Effort' (with the least amount of effort):

1. Accept people, circumstances and events as they are in this moment

You can't change the moment, but you can change the future if you accept the moment. When confronted with any challenge, remind yourself, 'This moment is as it should be, because the entire universe is as it should be.'

2. Take full and personal responsibility

...for each of your decisions and for your situation. Never blame anything or anyone, including yourself, your decisions or your actions. Every problem is an opportunity to take this moment and transform it into a greater benefit.

3. Relinquish the need to defend your point of view

In defencelessness, you remain open to all points of view, not rigidly attached to one of them; embracing improvements and gifts that are always there but most can't see.

Start Now sound bite

When in flow you will spontaneously make better decisions due to a lack of friction and tension, and heightened intuition. Do not push too hard, let go to grow and use the 'Law of Least Effort', just like nature does, to materialize all that you are worthy of (which is infinite).

53
Vision & values

You will know if you've read *Life Leverage* and *Money*, that I strongly believe clarity of and alignment with your vision and values makes all decisions and actions spontaneously clear to you. It takes no effort to link your task or big decision to your vision and values, to inherently know your single right action.

If you are not gaining clarity on the vision and purpose of your life, what gets you inspired with least effort and the unique talents and passions that you bring to life, then check out *Life Leverage* and do the simple vision and values exercises. This is a very important action. This will be an action that will negate 80% of other decisions you have to make, as they will cascade away once you have clarity of what is most important to you in your life.

When you have hard, important, overwhelming decisions to make, a quick check against your vision and values will give you instant clarity and right action focus. You are already living according to your values, you just don't know it. You may not be linking the tasks you're struggling with to your values and how the actions serve them.

If it's important enough to you, you'll find a way. If not, you'll find an excuse.

Values

Your values are the things that are most important to you in your life, in organized priority. Family, health, business, hobbies, passions, professions, travel, freedom and other such concepts are values. No one else has the same values as you in the same order of priority because, if two people on the planet were the same, one wouldn't be needed. You are an inspired genius in being you because no one else is like you. When you are authentic and living according to your values, you are the best you that anyone else could be, in flow, focused and spontaneously prioritized.

Vision

Your vision is the ultimate, life-long manifestation of your values lived with inspiration. Your vision is the roadmap for your life, guiding you in each moment through crossroads, tough choices, setbacks, diversions and transient periods, where you lack clarity and experience confusion. *Without a vision and purpose, you have no purpose.* This goes some way to explaining why so many people wrestle through looking for the meaning of life. I believe the meaning of life is to find your true unique purpose so that you add value to humanity and therefore evolve the species.

Start Now sound bite

If in doubt of the right action, check your big, hard or important decision against your vision and values. Link the action to serving them and you will spontaneously focus and prioritize.

54
Manage your inner bas-tard

Most people are ruled by their emotions. Some their whole life, others from time to time when they lose control and flip out. Have you ever reacted angrily or without due care, only to regret it later? It could be getting angry with someone, sending an email-missile back in response to how you read an email from them (wrongly), or you jumped to a conclusion only to feel stupid afterwards. We all have. None of us are perfect. It isn't you, it's your inner bas-tard; the emotionally childish, volatile version of you.

To manage your emotions well is to master your life. To be a slave to them is to always be vulnerable, out of control and pushing people and success away from you. These inner emotions can taunt and curse you. They can be all of your fears and past baggage and people who've hurt you merged into the nagging, petulant voice of your inner bas-tard.

Managing your emotions is not about denying your feelings but observing them and taking a moment to try to understand them. Why are you feeling and reacting this way? What purpose do these volatile emotions serve?

Here are 10 strategies you can test in your own life to understand, manage, control and master your emotions, to master your decisions, actions and results:

1. Observe the emotion

Take yourself out of the emotion and, like another voice or person inside you, watch without judgement. 'Oh, that is an interesting reaction, Rob. Look at what your inner bas-tard did there!'

2. What is beneath the emotion or reaction?

Where is it coming from? What, in you, is making you react like this?

3. Why is it persisting?

What are you not learning? What triggers it?

4. What is the feedback that you need to own to grow through it?

What do you need to improve to master it, by controlling your reactions?

5. How does this emotion benefit you?

What are the hidden benefits and lessons of inner bas-tard?

6. Isolate yourself

Go to a space alone where your emotion can't disrupt your life or others at that moment, until it subsides. By all means let your inner bas-tard flip out, then burn out. Then consider your next move with a balanced view.

7. Have a friend-punch-bag

Have a go-to person you trust who is discreet and will not judge you. Ask them, 'Can I have a rant please?' Then let rip. Let the bas-tard out. Exorcize that demon! Once it's out you may feel a lot better. The storing and suppressing of strong emotions can lead to passive aggressive behaviours, a full melt down or, worse, illness.

8. Have trusted counsel

Good friends, advisors and mentors who you can talk with and who are qualified to give smart advice are great for you to bounce ideas off. Especially those who've experienced your inner bas-tard becoming your outer bas-tard.

9. Wait before you make a rash or emotional (or any) decision

10. Read, listen to and attend courses from the top experts...

...in the fields related to the persistent challenge you have. Learn from the best.

Start Now sound bite

Manage your inner bas-tard by allowing and observing your feelings and simply noticing them. Your inner bas-tard is not you; it is the volatile, emotional version of you. Take a breath, a little time alone or with trusted counsel then, once the emotion (bas-tard) has subsided, you can make good, rational decisions by following one of more of the 10 points.

55
Making *really* hard decisions

This book is not just about making quick decisions, but *smart* decisions. I hope you don't have to make (m)any life-threatening decisions. From time to time in your life you will be faced with really hard decisions, no matter how many strategies are covered in this book.

Go back through the decision-making strategies that you've found the most useful so far in this book. Perhaps the ones that you previously struggled with or didn't even know about. This could be 'The law of proportional decision making' (Chapter 48), 'Pros & Cons' (Chapter 43), 'Intuition vs. information' (Chapter 40), 'De-risk the downside' (chapter 41), 'Vision & values' (Chapter 53) or more. Once you have covered these, and still find the decision hard, then move on to the points below.

0. Step 'zero' is to accept that it *is* a really tough decision

...and as such there may not be a right (or clear) answer. This also means there may not be a wrong answer.

1. Don't search for the right answer, search for the best answer given the circumstances

2. The right thing can often be the hardest decision you're facing

Whilst that sounds obvious, the decision is probably hard because you don't want to make the hard decision. So therein lies the potential answer.

3. What would you advise a friend in this situation?

Take yourself outside of yourself to give a clear, balanced and caring view. What would you advise someone to do who you really cared about, in this tough situation?

4. Seek out others who've faced this really hard choice

People have been there and been through the pain. Share openly how you are feeling and the challenges you are having. If they felt them too, what they did do?

5. Tap into your higher power

Whether religion, spirituality, meditation, infinite intelligence or visualization is your thing, call on your highest power with all your faith and the answer should come to you.

6. Do what is most right, kind and caring for the most people involved

Mums who want a career have to make hard decisions. Leaving a partner when you have family and financial commitments could be a hard decision. Terri Irwin, widow of Crocodile Hunter Steve Irwin, knew her husband took risks. Jackie Kennedy married JFK knowing the risks. It's wise to remember that many have had decisions much harder than, and outcomes much worse than, us.

Start Now sound bite

From time to time you may have to make really tough decisions. These should not be done flippantly. Go back and practise the decision-making techniques you found the most useful, then move on to the six steps of making tough decisions above. Do what is right. Seek out others who've faced these hard decisions. Often, you just need to face up to, and do, hard things you know you have to do.

SECTION 8

Commitments

Decisions are better made and then stuck to, if you fully commit. Chopping and changing and stopping and starting not only lead you around in circles chasing your tail, but reduce trust in you through a lack of consistency. Making commitments, sticking to them, and becoming known for sticking to your commitments will help you get more of the right things decided and done and help other people have trust in you.

It takes just as much energy to commit as it does to give up. It takes as much energy to stop and start and stop and start as it does to push through some challenges and stay committed. Some people are naively looking for complete freedom but, the reality is, no matter who you are, we are all accountable to someone: a boss, our kids, our partner, customers, shareholders, staff, managers, followers and fans. And we need it, despite telling ourselves we don't like it. This section will help you be clearer to make the right commitments and then stick to them.

56
Strengths, weaknesses & mistakes

It is said by many that it is OK to make a mistake, but never to make the same mistake twice. I'd like to challenge this by saying that most of us make the same mistakes over and over and over again. We also make the same successes over and over and over again. This is because we are who we are. Our habits and personality traits are ingrained in us deeply, more so the older we get and, as such, we will repeat our patterns.

This can be both a good thing and a bad thing. Making the same bad, stupid mistakes over and over and not learning from them has an obvious drawback. But in balance of this is the repeated pattern of our strengths. No one can be good at all things and, therefore, not bad at all things as there are too many things and we all have our own unique values and purpose. There is a good case for focusing mostly on your strengths and outsourcing your weaknesses to someone else, instead of spending much time and energy changing what can't be changed.

I have cycled around in my thought process of where we should focus our time, learning and effort to improve. Should we focus on strengthening our strengths so we become the very best? Should we focus on strengthening our weaknesses so that we don't fail making the same mistakes? I think it depends on what those strengths and weaknesses are, what systems, people and resources we have available, and how we get our pleasure, results and money.

If I could suggest a sweet spot, it would be to focus most of your time and resource on your strengths, to be the very best you can be. Then you spend a small amount of your time upskilling your big weaknesses to a satisfactory level.

You won't become the best putting too much time into try-ing to fix your weaknesses, as it will pull your strengths down. You'll end up becoming average/good at lots of things, which can lead to not much of anything. None of the best in the world in their art were average/good at everything (with, per-haps, the exception of successful entrepreneurs, who often need to be good generalists). I got good at many things and great at nothing, which is why I ultimately failed in previous vocations and activities. I humbly succeeded (so far) as an entrepreneur because I could be a generalist but, even in this endeavour, the billionaires and change makers usually have one or two huge skills, that other mere mortals can't match.

It is important to up-skill your big weaknesses to a satisfac-tory level. You can't be terrible at managing your emotions, or people, and get away with it. Fundamental skills that are essential to progress must be at a basic or above level. Once you are there, outsource everything else to partners, staff, VAs and systems more suited and proficient at your weaknesses.

This will cover all bases the best way you can. It will stop your one big weakness from breaking everything, yet at the same time allow you to achieve in that area through leverage. You then focus most of your time in your areas of great skill and enjoyment. This liberates you, allows you to rise to the top fast and outsource the things you hate, that usually consume your time, energy and well-being.

It took me 26 years of my life to work this out and I finally got it thanks to my amazing business partner, Mark Homer. Having had the chance to reverse engineer our partnership so far (started in 2006), I realize I kept jumping from thing to thing to thing to thing. I seemed to be able to get quite good quite quickly, but then sabotaged myself moving on to the next thing. Usually my one big weakness would compromise my many (yet very thin) talents, or even some individual things

I got quite good at. When I met him at a local property event, purely by chance, I found him strange at first. Even weird and eccentric. I know the feelings were mutual!

I realized a few months in that, not only was he great at what I was a disaster at, but he actually LOVED doing those things. At first. I thought I better shut up in case he gave those tasks and projects back to me! I realized that I was allowing him the freedom to do as he loved, because I was doing the things he hated. He realized the same thing in reverse. We were allowing and leveraging each other to both do more of things we loved, and less of the things we hated. Those things we both hated were being done lovingly by each other.

This has a huge compounded effect. I am not saying it is perfect, there are challenges in having partners, and in outsourcing and letting go, but it was the formula for both of us to grow not just 10×, but 100× more than we would have done on our own. Neither of us has got to change; we can be comfortable being who we are and that is really liberating. We can both leverage each other. I even let Mark do all my worrying for me and outsource that to him(!), so I can sleep like a baby. In return, I take the trolls and haters and protect him from them.

Start Now sound bite

Focus most of your time building on your strengths, a little time getting your big weaknesses to a satisfactory level only, and outsource, leverage and partner on the rest. Don't try to fix all your mistakes as what you are bad at is balanced out by what you're great at. You are who you are, and that is great. Most of your personality has been formed, so go with that flow rather than trying to completely change who you are.

57
Stick to your word

Your word is more than a fleeting comment. Take it very seriously. People will believe you when you give it to them. *Your word is a measure of your worth*. Your word (kept) builds trust, credibility, goodwill, equity, lend-worthiness, referrals and a reputable, share-worthy brand.

As you are only as good as your word, breaking it will make you seem flaky, untrustworthy (even if you're nice) and a letdown. You may not have intended to, but someone could really have relied on you sticking to your word and, in not doing so, you could have made things very difficult for them. Small things can lead to big things so missed appointments, late cancellations and standing people up can turn into much bigger issues. If you start with the smaller commitments, it will build your commitment muscle for the bigger things.

It is said that discipline is doing what you know is right, no matter how hard, even when you don't feel like it. Wayward emotions, a lack of energy, enthusiasm or impatience may all tempt you to back down on your commitments. Here are some ways to get better at making the right decisions in the moment that help you stick to your word. *What goes around comes around, and what you put out you bring about*:

1. Don't over commit or give your word out too easily

Take time to consider giving your word. Don't just say 'yes' to everything. Don't say 'yes' out of guilt or not wanting to let someone down. Be as serious about giving your word as you are sticking to it and you won't get yourself into tricky situations. Only say 'yes' to things that you're passionate about, or that you know you will do, or that *have* to be done.

2. Think how you will feel and how it will be afterwards

Usually a bigger commitment feels way better afterwards than something that was easy. *The harder at the start, the sweeter at the end.* So think, and even try to feel, how you will feel afterwards, when you are tempted to break your word. Then when you stick by your word, and feel great, pat yourself on the back. Have a nice word with yourself; it was challenging but you got through it and now you feel great. This trains you to tackle and enjoy even bigger commitments.

3. Know (and call back to) WHY you gave your word

Sometimes, we say 'yes' to a lot of things but we forget why we said 'yes' in the first place. We can lose passion and direction, and then quit. Before you cancel anything, try to remember why you originally said 'yes', and what the upside was that will help you endure the challenges.

4. Respect other people (their time, feelings)

Your time and feelings are not more valuable than others. Respect others' time much as you respect and want to protect your own. Everyone has priorities and a 'to do' list each day too. Cancelling on them disrupts their day and life, and that's not fair. You don't want people ruining your schedule so don't do it to others.

5. Don't beat yourself up, pay it back

It's not that you're a bad person if you break your word, so don't beat yourself into a pulp. Have a little rule to learn from breaking your word, why you did it, and then 'buy back' your character, reputation and integrity with an act of kindness, generosity or hard work. Go beyond your original commitment. Give more. Do more. Not only does this regain your reputation, it also supports you on your journey to being a good person. When you mess up, be more generous, and you will win people over even more, because they say it's not what happens to you, but how you react to it that counts.

Keeping your word to yourself is not just about your reputation, brand and trust, it is about respecting yourself too. It is about being confident and authentic and saying 'yes' and 'no' to the right things. Your words are the building blocks of your existence and they reflect your integrity. Either sticking to or going back on your word builds your character up and down accordingly.

Start Now sound bite

Be careful and strategic about what you commit to. When you are clear, focus on WHY you are committing to it and then commit. Stick to your word and your commitments because they are your brand, reputation, goodwill, equity, lend-worthiness and, ultimately, trust. Refer back to why you made the commitment if you wobble.

58
(How to) Do what you know

To know and not to do is not to know. Much of the time, you know what you need to do. So why aren't you doing it? This chapter is designed as a quick reference to 'have a word with yourself'. You don't need new information or secrets or fancy techniques. You just need to GOYA and JFDI:

1. Stop thinking. Start doing

To think too long about doing a thing often becomes its undoing. Don't blow it out of proportion or get overwhelmed by its size. Stop putting it off. Start small.

2. Get rid of all distractions and isolate yourself

Make sure you have all the resources you need to get the job done. Get RID of all the things that could interrupt you and get on with it.

3. Get out of the void

Get off the fence. Get out of no man's land. Decide now. Decide something. Then make it better as you go along.

4. Start early and go BIG

Start as soon as you can so you don't have a chance to talk yourself out of it. Just START. As soon as you get up, or get ready, start. Start with the biggest, most important task and get stuck in. Do not fluff around and posturize on small things.

5. Eat that frog

Do the hard things first and fast. Attack them. Make the hard call. Do the thing you've been putting off. You'll feel great and get good momentum tackling the hard stuff; and you stop it nagging away at you, which only consumes more time.

6. Don't look backwards

You've made your decision, now look forwards. Don't second-guess yourself or look at other decisions you could have made. Or other people. You've committed, now stick to it.

7. Stop asking for more opinions

Enough! You've already done that. You know what to do, so simplify your decision by reducing opinion and influence so you can increase focus.

8. Stop talking. Stop making excuses. GOYA and JFDI.

Start Now sound bite

Follow one or more of the steps in this short, sharp chapter because you know what you have to do, so just go and do it.

59
Make that decision right

The weight of a decision should not be more on making the decision, but making the decision *right*. A good decision can be made bad by bad management of the actions. Conversely a bad decision could be made good with continued good decisions and right actions.

If you are on the fence about a decision, then it is a 50/50 chance of you making the right (or wrong) decision. You could argue that it really doesn't matter that much which decision you make. Once you have made your decision you focus, prioritize and set about getting (sh)it done. As every decision simply leads to another one, the last decision becomes an even less relevant distant memory, and you get another chance to make a good decision to get closer to your outcome.

Try not to have a plan B. If you have a plan B, you have something to fall back on, which might distract yourself from a full forward focus towards plan A. Most wrongs can be made right. Once you have made the initial trigger decision, looking back will only hold you back. Look forward, even if you have to fail forward.

Believe in yourself that you will find a way. If anyone can do it, as long as it is humanly possible, you can too. Your faith in the outcome and belief in your ability to find your way there will outweigh retrospective bad and good decisions every time. This should be where 90% of your time, energy and focus go, not on a single decision. You have it in your power and control to make your decision the right decision.

As you read this next section, see if you can guess who this person is:

- ☐ He failed in business at age 21
- ☐ His mum and sister died
- ☐ He was defeated in a legislative race at age 22
- ☐ He failed again in business at age 24
- ☐ He had a total nervous breakdown and was bedridden for 6 months
- ☐ His sweetheart died at age 26
- ☐ He went bankrupt
- ☐ His first son died at age 4
- ☐ He had a nervous breakdown at age 27
- ☐ He lost a congressional race at age 34
- ☐ He lost a congressional race at age 36
- ☐ His second son died at age 12
- ☐ He lost a senatorial race at age 45
- ☐ He failed in an effort to become vice-president at age 47
- ☐ He lost a senatorial race at age 47
- ☐ He was elected President of the United States at age 52

That man was Abraham Lincoln.

It is fair to say that Mr Lincoln was a great man. He made the decision to follow his dream and take all the necessary actions and tough decisions, even when having the most horrific luck and awful things happening around him. I truly admire the human spirit Mr Lincoln showed.

Here is another person who made a decision 'against all odds' but made that decision right. Can you guess who she is?

- ☐ Her mum left her when she was 8
- ☐ She was teased at school for wearing dresses made of potato sacks

- ☐ She was raped at 9
- ☐ She was molested by a family friend, uncle and cousin
- ☐ She ran away because of sexual abuse at home
- ☐ She became pregnant at 14
- ☐ Her son died after birth
- ☐ She was hired at a local black radio station to do the news part time
- ☐ She became the youngest news anchor and first black female news anchor

Since then she interviewed Michael Jackson, which became the third most watched interview ever. She became the first African American woman among the 50 most generous people, having given over $400 million to educational causes. She got her own network which made $300 million a year. She is now worth $3 billion and even has her own street, 'Oprah Winfrey Way'.

Wow. Like Lincoln, Oprah made tough decisions and went through extreme hardship and forged her way to being one of *the* most inspirational people on the planet today. When incredibly successful Sheryl Sandberg, of Google and Facebook, lost her husband at just age 47, she decided to use this grief to help others deal with adversity and loss.

Start Now sound bite

Whatever decision you make, commit to it and make that decision right. There will be tough times ahead, but many inspiring people have had very hard times and gone on to greatness. You can do whatever you put your mind to, despite your challenges, by deciding and putting your resources and focus on that decision. You can, and will, make your decision right.

60
Do the right thing, right

In any decision, there is usually one right action above all others. When you trust yourself and your intuition, this comes to you with the least amount of conscious effort. Deepak Chopra calls this 'Spontaneous Right Action' (SRA):

> 'There is only one choice, out of the infinity of choices available in every second, that will create happiness for you as well as for those around you…Spontaneous right action is the right action at the right moment. It's the right response to every situation as it happens.'

In this decisive state, your thoughts and actions are fully aligned with universal laws. 'They are 'right' actions, because they are appropriate to the time and circumstances and support evolution at every level of creation. The actions are 'spontaneous' because it is not necessary for the conscious mind to calculate and be aware of every possible influence it can have in time and space before choosing to act'. Imagine your conscious mind having to evaluate those 35,000 decisions a day; in fact don't, it will blow your mind!

The impulse for natural, spontaneous, intuitive behaviour is beyond logic. 'One simply acts in a natural, easy manner… operating within unbounded awareness automatically producing action that is in harmony with nature.'

I believe we all have this 'natural' decision-making ability within us. Some people call it 'trusting your gut', others 'following your heart' and others the 'infinite intelligence'. It is a sense we all have. I also believe you can improve your ability to make and follow SRAs with more faith and trust in yourself. Doubts, debates and critical analysis can block SRAs.

I've made some mistakes in my life, but never when trusting my sense of SRA. While walking in a crowd to a Liverpool football game, I found a wad of cash on the floor, around £200. I picked it up and my critical brain went into overdrive of all the decisions I could make, and the justifications for keeping the money. Who would know? It was so busy, where could I hand it in? I didn't want to miss the game.

In another situation at Peterborough Queensgate shopping centre, on a packed Saturday afternoon, a big, strong tattooed man was beside himself with worry, shouting out and screaming a boy's name. People were ignoring him and walking by. I could have done the same. I had things to do. What if he was threatening?

Logic is a way of using the intellect to gain understanding. It is valid, but not as much for deeper, instinctive decisions. SRAs emerge quickly when you trust and listen, through an infinite possibility of decisions and, as such, give powerful clarity and focus. There is no chance to procrastinate or be overwhelmed. Whether you tend to be more spiritual, or you have more critical thinking, we all have an inherent sense of what is the right thing to do. We simply have to move out of the way of our resistance to the natural right action.

Handing in the money to the box office before the Liverpool game felt amazing. I really could have done with the money back then, but I knew the decision was the right one.

I sensed true fear in the tattooed man. As my wife was expecting our first baby, I felt his pain and knew the right thing to do. I sensed that a lost boy might be at a games shop, so went to the closest one and saw a young boy looking at the new game releases, but also lost and worried. I asked him if he'd lost his dad and he burst out crying. I held his arm and weaved him through and against the mass of shoppers. The crowds seemed to open up once we got to his dad. When they saw each other they both cried and grabbed each other in the longest hug I've ever seen. Then they both grabbed and squeezed me with the hardest hug I've ever had. When they finally let me go and thanked me for the 400th time, I walked home and I felt amazing, and convinced of SRAs.

Start Now sound bite

Spontaneous right action (SRA) is the one, single, natural right action — from the infinite amount of possibilities — to allow the least resistance for nature to present the natural outcome. This relies less on logic and more on intuition and faith in yourself and nature. It is always within you, you feel it and it requires the least amount of effort.

61
Problem solvers rule the world

As well as having infinite solutions, there are infinite problems to solve in the universe, balancing the pull between order and chaos. Problems can be seen as resistance and difficulties, as most people perceive them, or they can be seen as the natural path to solutions, much like mistakes can be perceived as failures or as a step closer to the solution.

If I am struggling to see the upsides of a problem or challenging situation, or perhaps wishing it away instead of working it away, I like to imagine a stereotypical techy computer geek. I perceive that they love hacking into a deep problem. It's like the bigger the challenge, the more fun they have trying to solve it. Who needs sleep?! Or imagine a scientist trying to create an antidote or cure for a disease. They don't throw their hands up in the air and their toys out of the pram and cry 'fuck this, it doesn't work. I hate it. Screw the world. I'm going home'.

Solving great problems is as much a mindset as it is a skill set. No one knows how to solve problems at first, otherwise they would be a solution, not a problem. All of us, no matter how smart or experienced – master or disaster; beginner or winner; Steve Jobs or no jobs – go into a problem from the same level starting position. *Your attitude is as important as your aptitude.*

The two most extreme reactions and applications to a problem are:

Scenario A. Victim. Defeated. Why me? I'm beaten. Wish it away. Avoid it. Pain.

Scenario B. Bring it on. Step up. I can do this. This is my chance. Big potential solution. I love a challenge.

Because most people veer towards Scenario A, problem solvers have dramatically increased value in society. Those who solve big and meaningful problems become leaders and gain faith, fans and followers (who often veer towards Scenario A). In many cases, these problem-solvers-turned-leaders encourage and inspire others to become problem solvers and leaders. Your value to society and the legacy you leave, as well as the wealth and success you attract, is directly linked to the scale, frequency, volume and meaningfulness of the problems you continue to solve.

If you analyse every meaningful invention, cure or advancement in technology or society, you will see they were all riddled with difficulties that the creators and innovators saw as challenges. Sometimes they kept going and got a stroke of luck or intervention. Sometimes they kept reviewing, tweaking and repeating until they struck gold. Often people died in the progression of science and medicine. For example, pacemakers were initially bulky, external units which required the use of mains power, as battery technology had not yet advanced sufficiently to allow implantation. Over many years and progressive problem solving, Wilson Greatbatch managed to miniaturize and package the device.

My mate Wilson puts his success down to persistence, grit and knowing that with every one solution which didn't work, he was one step closer: 'Nine things out of ten don't work', he says, but emphasises that, 'The tenth one will pay for the other nine'. Notice also he calls the problem a 'solution', not a problem.

Great companies, innovators and leaders continue to solve problems that make the lives of the masses easier, faster, better and more convenient. *It doesn't take genius, it takes an attitude of accepting, tackling and even enjoying problems.* Problem solvers rule the world, and the rest follow in hope, faith and gratitude that their problems will be solved for them. And they pay for those solutions.

Start Now sound bite

You don't have to be a genius to solve meaningful problems, you just have to have the mindset before the skill set. Your attitude to solving problems dictates your aptitude. There are infinite problems to solve that lead to infinite solutions, so problems are inherent in solutions. Get stuck in, stand up and tackle big problems and you will increase in value and self-worth. You will become a great leader who inspires other leaders. Problem solvers rule the world.

SECTION 9
Conclusion

62
Investing time (not wasting it)

If you have to keep starting again and again (and deciding again and again) then you spend, duplicate and waste more and more time. Decisions and actions get easier, faster and more intuitive in the future if you carry forward lessons, systems and best practices. *Each decision is not only a chance to do the right thing now, but an investment in doing the right things, better, in the future.*

There are five ways to utilize your time. WISLR. This *almost* spells a memorable word to help you retain it in your memory:

- ☐ Waste
- ☐ Invest
- ☐ Spend
- ☐ Leverage
- ☐ Recover

Waste

Spend as little of your time as possible wasting this precious, limited resource you have. Distractions, procrastination, debates, arguments, duplication, defending your position, excuses, blaming, justifying and seeking attention *all* drain your time and energy. Be ruthless and minimize these as much as you can.

Invest

Invest time into building assets that give a recurring, residual and/or passive, long-term benefit. 'Spend' the time once and 'earn' on it forever. Time that gives security, freedom, wealth and leverage. This could be property, stocks, business, systems, information and IP, leadership, education, staffing, outsourcing, time with loved ones, philanthropy and anything that aligns with your values.

Spend

Time spent can be valuable *or* distracting, depending on how you use it. You can spend time with loved ones or smart people. You can be earning a great living doing something you love. Or you could be spending hours on the Internet or selling your soul in a job you hate. Be aware and wise in how you spend your time, moving as much of it into invested time and as little as possible into wasted time.

Leverage

Leveraged time is the continued, recurring benefit that builds on invested time. A system that automates a process you don't have to perform, or a book or podcast created in the past, or a staff member, outsourcer or even a Christmas No.1 (think Slade) 'leverages' time. *You don't have to be there, do it or touch it, and it still liberates time and generates outcomes and incomes.*

Recover

Time to recharge, plan, think, make space, observe, calibrate and be present to breathe in everything that gives life colour and meaning. This can be strategy, planning, setting goals, holidays, time with loved ones, hobbies, meditation, Netflix or sleep. I have seen more importance in this measure of time as I have moved towards age 40.

Start Now sound bite

Life is short. Blink and we're gone. Do not waste it. Value it. Protect it. Remember WISLR to reduce wastage and increase leverage to do more of what you love, when you love, where you love and with whom you love.

63
What if you don't decide to decide?
Part 2.

What won't you achieve?
Where will you not go?
What might you regret?
Who will you not love?
Who might you not become?
What will you not leave behind?

These are all questions that could remain unanswered, that you may have to live with the rest of your life, if you don't start making some decisions fast. There's nothing wrong with peering into the future to see all the things you could have done if you don't 'Start Now. Get Perfect Later' to stir a little pain inside yourself to commit yourself.

Bronnie Ware, an Australian nurse who spent years working in palliative care, caring for patients in the last 12 weeks of their lives; recorded their dying epiphanies and then wrote a book, *The Top Five Regrets of the Dying: A Life Transformed by the Dearly Departing*. The top five regrets she learned from the dying:

☐ I wish I cared less of what others think
☐ I wish I didn't worry so much
☐ I wish I took better care of myself
☐ I wish I didn't take life for granted
☐ I wish I lived in the now

Other regrets of people facing death are:

☐ I wish I'd had the courage to live a life true to myself, not the life others expected of me
☐ I wish I hadn't worked so hard
☐ I wish I'd had the courage to express my feelings
☐ I wish I had stayed in touch with my friends
☐ I wish that I had let myself be happier

Perhaps the worse regret of all is regret itself. Regretting what you could have done, what you could have achieved and who you could have become. I do not share this to scare you but to shock you into action and decision.

It is a worthy exercise once a year to do the 'Regret Test'. Project forward and peer into the end of your life as a bystander by your bed. What regrets might you have that you share with Bronnie Ware writing her book, or your children holding your hand? Write them down, file them where you can refer to them easily and often, and *make sure you live every moment now making the decisions and taking the actions that will leave you with as few regrets as possible.*

> 'Think of all the years passed by in which you said to yourself "I'll do it tomorrow", and how the gods have again and again granted you periods of grace of which you have not availed yourself. It is time to realize that you are a member of the Universe, that you are born of Nature itself, and to know that a limit has been set to your time.'
>
> *Marcus Aurelius*

I can't believe how quickly I've approached 40. I am nearing half my life. I pissed away much of my late teens and early 20s. No regrets because it is the path that has led me to the here and now, with you. But those seven years in the wilderness I'll never get back, so I carry that forward. I hope that you take your regrets, lessons and challenges and carry them forward with you as motivation to rise up and be the person you know you are meant to be. You have amazing gifts and talents. The world needs them. People are lost. They need your guidance. *They need you to be the person you are meant to be so that they can become the person they want to be.*

Shine your light on them. Lead the way. *Don't wish it were easier, become better.*

David J. Lieberman, Ph.D., author of *The Science of Happiness* calls happiness, 'the continual progression toward meaningful objectives'. It is not just the rest and play that makes us happy. Perhaps the times in your life when you were the happiest were in the form of huge relief after you got a hard and nasty task or project behind you. Or when you saw the things you'd been building or creating or writing for a long time *finally* become a reality. Or when you hadn't seen your family or loved ones for a long while.

Find happiness in taking on bigger and tougher decisions knowing you are growing through challenges and solving more important, meaningful problems.

I hope I have served you well. Here's to your ever-growing health, wealth, happiness and decisiveness.

End Now sound bite

When all is said and done, more is said than done. It's never too late to start, but it's always too late to wait. To know and not to do is not to know, so just go. Thank you. I am grateful to you. I believe in you. GOYA and JFDI. Start Now. Get Perfect Later.

Glossary

Ducks in a row A quintessentially English phrase that means to get everything prepared, planned and ready to start. I know, us Brits can be strange.

GOYA Get Off Your Arse (or Ass).

IGT (Income Generating Task) Highest revenue generating tasks or activity.

Inner bas-tard The voice in your head that taunts you. The fears and past baggage and people who've hurt you all merged into a nagging, petulant voice that makes you randomly behave like a total twat. And then you regret it later.

JFDI Just Fuckin' Do It.

KRA (Key Result Area) Highest return and value areas of your business, role and life.

SRA (Spontaneous Right Action) The single right action for the single best outcome.

WISLR Acronym for measuring time: Wasted. Invested. Spent. Leveraged. Recover(ed).

WTAF No way. Never. You can't be serious. I'm speechless.

WTF Really? You must be kidding me.